DOG ABOUT TOWN

For Kyle, Forest and Cookie X

LOUISE GLAZEBROOK

Illustrated by Ping Zhu

DOG ABOUT TOWN

How to raise a happy dog in the city

hardie grant books
MELBOURNE · LONDON

CONTENTS

INTRODUCTION

This book has been my dream for a long time. I am a dog trainer and behaviourist and I live and work in the city. I live the life my clients lead, so I understand how hard it can be to work out what is best for my dog in this environment.

Urban living is wonderful – it is diverse, interesting, noisy and, most of all, there is always something happening, which I personally adore. That isn't to say that I don't yearn for a secluded cottage by the sea as a weekend getaway every now and then! However, my day-to-day time is built around the complexities of a city. My dog, Cookie, a seven-year-old deaf English bulldog, is also known as The Unicorn as she is white with a brown spot perfectly positioned on her head. She has only ever known what it is like to live in London. She thinks that buses driving past every couple of minutes are normal, and it's sometimes hard to remember that I've raised a dog in one of the toughest, most stimulating environments that is humanly possible.

Now living a life in the city certainly isn't for every person and it isn't for every dog. There are some dogs that excel at it and there are others that really suffer and hate it. The selection of your dog is key to making your life in town as a dog owner as easy as possible. You may be thinking of moving out of town in the next few years, but if that is still some time away, for now you need to focus on your immediate situation. (Some of my clients are lucky enough to live in the city five days a week and in the country two days a week. That for me sounds idyllic but isn't how most of us manage to operate.)

Urban dogs will usually have less space to live, may not have a garden, will travel by public transport, will see hundreds of dogs in a month and will be expected to accept everything they come into contact with from pub to train to kids scootering past and high levels of background noise. But if their needs are met, they can lead happy lives in the city, and bring joy to an owner's home.

This book is not designed as a training manual, instead it's here to help you navigate the unique challenges and pleasures your city throws at you and your dog. It will encourage you to think outside of your world and see things a little differently: to get down on your dog's level and see what he sees, understand what he may find hard to accept and the reasons why. It will show you how to find, select and introduce a dog into your city life, and help you achieve a lifestyle that will suit you both.

1.

FINDING YOUR CITY DOG

WHY DO YOU WANT A DOG?

There are a million and one reasons why people decide to take on a dog. Here are just some of the many I have heard over the years:

'I had a dog growing up and always wanted a four-legged companion of my own.'

'I want my children to grow up with a respect for animals. Having a dog, they'll get as much love back as they put in.'

'I want a dog to join me on my daily run. It will make it fun!'

'I work from home, and want a companion to keep me company and get me out the house.'

'We have been together for a while now and feel ready to take on the responsibility of a dog. We are desperate to share our lives with one.'

'When I think of all the dogs in shelters it's just heartbreaking. I want to offer one a home.'

I have worked with the full spectrum of city people who already own dogs or who are about to find one. The reasons vary hugely and it's always interesting to understand why owners wanted to bring a dog into their life – the reason has a huge impact on the type of dog that they end up with. Spend time discussing with friends, family, and your partner why you actually want a dog.

Is it for companionship, to go running with you, to have someone to come home to or because you have always dreamt of owning a particular dog? Whatever that reason, you now need to decide if you are able to give that dog what it requires.

If you think about it, no dog would ever place an advert looking for an owner that said: 'Wanted: owner who is out of the house for twelve hours every day, who wants to go to the pub after work and not see their dog very much. Very little exercise or stimulation offered, and hours spent alone during the week guaranteed.' Unfortunately this situation arises all too often in our cities.

You see, owning a dog is not just about what *we* want. The first and most important rule of owning a dog is that it is not okay to leave your dog for long periods of time. This especially needs to be considered by those living in urban areas, as life is busy, and fast paced and owners have lots to do every day.

For example, I once had a couple who came to my classes with two working cocker spaniel puppies. They worked full time and told me that they were going to get a dog walker to exercise their dogs for an hour a day. Yet the other ten hours they were at work and the dogs would be at home alone. They felt this was okay, in my opinion it definitely isn't.

If you work full time, a dog walker coming in for an hour every day isn't enough. I want all owners to be the focus of their dog's worlds. If there is someone at home for most of each day, if you can take your dog to work, if you can give your dog all the exercise and stimulation it needs – if you want it to truly be a member of your family – then you will be able to build a meaningful relationship together and give it a happy and healthy home, wherever you are.

WHAT BREED IS RIGHT FOR YOU?

When choosing a breed, a crucial consideration is that you live in a city or urban area. Country or small-townhomes may offer relative isolation from other houses, substantial gardens, they may be surrounded by fields, and it is likely that country-living dogs won't meet hundreds of others in the local park.

For the city dog and owner, life is different:

· City living means smaller homes, flats and apartments.
· They may not have a garden or outdoor space, meaning that the only place for the dog to go to the toilet is in public.
· The parks that you use and have access to will be busy places filled with dogs, kids, adults, bikes, joggers and much more.
· Many owners will not own a car, so the dog will need to use public transport such as the train, bus and Tube.
· Every street that you walk on is likely to be busy.
· Everywhere is very noisy.
· Dogs are often allowed into some pubs, shops, cafes and other venues, which is both good and bad.
· If your dog was bred to hunt or dig, it will take a great deal of input from you to enable them to naturally fulfil their 'purpose' in the city in a way that you are happy with.
· Every type of vehicle known to man will enter a city – bicycles, scooters, lorries, trains, buses, motor-bikes, trailers and caravans – and your dog will need to learn to ignore them all.

· You will most likely need to find a paid walker or carer to help you.

· There will be restricted areas where your dog can and cannot go, and where they can and cannot go off lead.

All in all, life in the city with a dog is hard. I talk from first-hand experience both from my own life and also from working with other owners' dogs. This is where your breed selection is key.

For example: if someone chose to remove a Border collie puppy from a farm and bring it into the city, to live in their two-bedroom apartment, where they went out to work all day and the most they could afford was a dog walker to do a one-hour street walk – they would have problems. There would be a lack of exercise and stimulation here for most dogs, but a working dog, designed to be out for hours each day and who is noise sensitive, fast and quick to learn would find themselves possibly in their worst nightmare. If a working dog's parents herded sheep, and there is now a distinct lack of sheep, we may end up with a collie herding children, adults or even cars. The instincts that were bred in for generations have to come out in some way. You cannot suppress them.

I have met this collie: he was taken from the farm, walked to work and back and chained to a radiator because he was herding staff in the office. Sadly, the owner wasn't willing to put in the work required, and the final straw came when it tried to herd cars and then bit an old lady who got in the way on the Euston Road. My only recommendation at that point was to rehome the dog out of the city as the dog was now a threat to public safety.

So it is very important that you look for a breed that will suit your lifestyle. Do not be fooled by cuteness, fluffiness or big ears! Ask yourself these essential questions below:

How much exercise do you want to do a day – and how much exercise can you realistically fit in each day? Be honest. Don't lie to yourself. I would say any breed of dog, no matter how tiny, needs to be taken out and about and exercised for at least two hours a day. If you are thinking of a malamute, husky-type breed, let's triple that. Can you fit that in every day of the year?

How often do you want to groom your dog or pay someone else to groom it? Cockapoos need grooming around every six weeks, whereas a shorthaired whippet need never see a groomer.

What do you want to do with your dog? I often see owners who have taken on dogs like a Jack Russell as they think they are small and so perfect for city living. They are only fine if you are a keen

runner and your dog can run with you. Size is not a reflection of activity. A Great Dane is huge but their exercise requirements are far less than a terrier.

Who do you live with and is this likely to change? If you are thinking of having children – even in five years' time – think about what sort of dog would work well with them, such as a Staffy, Labrador, Irish terrier, beagle or bulldog. There are many dogs that work brilliantly well with children, equally there are some which struggle that bit more, in my experience, such as Manchester terriers, Welsh and Lakeland terriers, or Border collies. Remember I am also talking about pairing children with a city environment. A family with two young children living on a farm is a very different set-up.

What is your tolerance to noise? If you don't want a dog that is yappy, don't buy a dog that is designed to alert, bark and defend, such as a dachshund, chihuahua, Hungarian vizsla or Rottweiler. In the same way, if you don't like snoring and snuffling avoid a pug, French bulldog or bulldog like the plague! Also consider your neighbours when it comes to the noise issue.

Do you really need a working breed, and can you give them enough stimulation? Think and think again about the heritage of the breed you are taking on. There are far more working-breed dogs

such as German shorthaired pointers, Hungarian vizslas, working cocker spaniels, and Patterdale terriers making their way into the city. It's lovely to see, if they are getting what they need, but I'm also seeing more of these dogs in rescue which indicates that people have found they chose the wrong dogs for their lifestyle. If you take on a dog designed to guard, bark, shake and tear things or to chase then you can't get frustrated when the dog starts doing these things. This is not the dog's fault, it is yours because you actively chose the wrong breed for you.

Here are some suggestions for breeds that can be great urban companions. You will, of course, still need to establish that they fit in with *your* urban lifestyle and, when you find a potential pooch, find out as much as you can about their parents (or temperament from the rescue centre) as you can. More on this later.

The Whippet A sighthound who is shorthaired, nimble and calm but who also loves to cuddle. They feel the cold, have calm dispositions and are eager to please. Originally bred to chase, so teaching recall is key.

Retired greyhounds Fabulous if you love a leggy friend who likes to snooze, but beware that with their heritage can often come sound sensitivities and strong chase instincts. Originally bred to race so they can do short distance very fast.

French bulldogs Compact, fun and a brilliant companion. Do not be told that they are lazy, they aren't. There can be breathing issues if not bred responsibly. Originally bred as companions.

Staffordshire bull terriers There are some superb examples in rescue and some great breeders. They make excellent family pets and live for some human

interaction. Originally bred as a bull baiter, this was out ruled in 1835 meaning that their breeding purpose totally changed.

Labrador If you love a bigger dog who needs lots of exercise but you don't have lots of steps to climb (as they get older they can have weak hips), Labradors are a breed worth considering. They are loyal, sturdy and very fun. Originally bred as a retriever, so it's an advantage if you love throwing a ball.

Miniature dachshund These dogs have soared in popularity due to their size and zest for life, but they can be noisy. Originally bred to go to ground after the likes of badgers and rabbits, which means they can be scent and nose driven.

Border terrier A joyful, enthusiastic dog that loves life and enjoys the challenges of the city. Originally bred to go to ground after foxes. Digging and chasing can be a favourite pastime.

Toy poodle Intelligent small dogs that love to please and learn tricks while taking city life in their stride. A descendant of a standard poodle, a water retriever, so do not be fooled by size and fluff – they were bed to be working dogs.

Lhasa apso A companion dog that is fluffy but not silly! They can be rather bark orientated so do bear this in mind. Originally bred as a watchdog.

Great Dane Aside from the size implications, for those that want a big dog but not masses of exercise, these are the gentle giants for you. They do not live a long life due to their size. Originally bred as a guarder and they can be nosy!

Cavalier King Charles There are a great deal of healthy issues to get past, but there are breeders doing a brilliant job. A calm and willing spaniel that loves to be around people and does not require a tremendous amount of exercise. Originally bred as a companion dog and they do love to lounge.

Beagle Generally a great size for city living and adored by owners who want a dog with personality but who loves to be part of team. Originally bred as scent hounds and this has never been bred out of them, so your dog will always have his nose to the ground.

Miniature schnauzer A robust dog that is quick and well suited to family and city life. They can be on alert and will bark, they also love to learn as much as you can teach them. Originally bred as a Jack of all trades from guarding, ratting and companionship, so choose your heritage lines carefully.

PUPPY VS RESCUE DOG

When you've decided on the best breeds for your lifestyle, the next decision is whether to find a puppy from a great breeder or a rescue dog. The third option is to find a rescue puppy!

PUPPY

We all know the gorgeous feeling of running your fingers through the hair of a puppy that smells of puppy breath. Many of us will also know the feeling of those needle teeth making contact with your hand as they learn about the world and what to bite. Let's talk about the joys and challenges of owning a puppy:

Joys of owning a puppy

· All the classic ideas fit in here. They are soft, cuddly, delicious, sleeping on your lap, warm bundles of fur.
· You are able to spend time researching and planning your new puppy addition which means you can try to choose a puppy that is perfect for you.
· It is wonderful to see your chosen puppy learning from you and succeeding at what you are teaching them.
· You can socialise them in all of the things that are key to your life in a city.
· You are able to build that relationship with your puppy from the day you take it home from the breeder.
· You become the person responsible for shaping that puppy for the future.
· You will start to become acquainted with your local drunks, late-night stop-outs and randoms as you roam the streets at 5 a.m. trying to get your dog to poo!

Challenges of owning a puppy

· It's really hard work with the toilet training, the biting, the sleep training, the lead walking, the recall and the socialisation.
· You need to be around during the day to socialise and toilet train your dog, which is tricky if you have a full-time job.
· You have to teach and train your dog to be the adult dog that you dreamt you would own.
· You need to adapt your life to be able to accommodate a puppy.
· It can sometimes reduce people to tears or to rehome their dog because it is that hard.
· You might end up having to redecorate your living room when your puppy decides that your skirting boards look like fair game.

RESCUE DOG

Joys of owning a rescue dog

· Usually these dogs are no longer puppies, so any issues or problem behaviours are out there and known about, and the previous owner/s will have discussed them with the rescue. If they came in as a stray, the rescue will have worked with the dog to assess them and advise potential owners.

· It's far easier to select a dog for your lifestyle as with an adult dog the rehoming centre can advise on exactly what that dog needs and if you are the right person to give it.
· It's unlikely you will need to toilet train a rescue dog.
· Rescue dogs are often (not always) great with recall – their first owner deserted them and they won't want you to do the same.
· You will know exactly how big, furry, long-legged, barky, attractive, ugly, affectionate that rescue dog is. There should be fewer surprises!

Challenges of owning a rescue dog

· Many (but not all) have issues that need working on.
· Some may have had some horrible experiences previously – usually caused by humans. Always remember that all behaviours are for a reason.

• Some will regress when they have spent time in kennels, so they may be anxious, worried about being separated from you or feel insecure.

• You are having to take on a dog that has associations and experiences you may know nothing about.

• Some, if they have come from a kennel for strays, will not have a history that the centre can go over with you. These dogs should be avoided if there are children in your home.

• The first four weeks of owning a rescue dog are called the honeymoon period, after this is when you often find new behaviours surfacing which is why it is crucial to have your boundaries in place from day one.

• As mentioned on page 18, rehoming your dog is an extremely unpleasant experience.

A RESCUE PUPPY

Now to many this option seems like the best of both worlds, as you take home a small bundle of fluff and have the opportunity to give a dog a second chance. Just bear in mind that essentially you still don't know any history, unless the mother is with the litter in the centre.

You must also take the time to look at the litter and how they interact with each other, as this can be very telling. I once met a litter of working-breed puppies whose mother had died. Even at just five weeks old the litter was incredibly scared and nervous. This was certainly not a litter that I would place in busy homes or homes with children. In the same way, I met a litter whose mother was rather aggressive and the litter were what I considered to be very rough with each other, displaying behaviour I didn't feel appropriate. They were a litter I would not have taken home either. Many may see it as cruel to reject a dog at this early stage of its life, but you have to go on the small amount of information you have and you mustn't be convinced by someone persuading you otherwise.

When looking for your perfect pooch, as well as choosing the breed right for your lifestyle, the individual dog must be right for your family. Whether it is a puppy, a rescue puppy or a rescue dog, if something about the dog (or its parents or its litter) doesn't seem right to you, you should not take it home. It is far worse to take a dog out of a rehoming centre for

six months and then return it than it is to leave it there a few more days while it finds the right home. The next two chapters look at this in more detail.

CHOOSING A BUNDLE OF PUPPY LOVE

The prospect of owning a puppy always gets people really excited, and quite rightly so. You are choosing a best friend to live with you for the next ten to fifteen years. That is an amazing prospect. Make sure you search for your puppy in a way that will set you up for future happiness.

It is a sad fact that huge numbers of dogs are being bred in the cruellest conditions imaginable, but there are also many puppies being bred in the best environment possible with all the right things being done at the right time. Now you have chosen the right breed for you, the next step is to find a breeder who looks like they are producing the best mate for you to share your life with.

In an urban environment it can be difficult to know where to look. It's not like the old days, where the local dog in the village would have a litter and your mum and dad would choose one because they knew and loved the mother dog. Now people are travelling far and wide to get a puppy, and in a city everything takes that bit more planning. With that in mind, I've created some dos and don'ts to help you get your puppy from a great breeder.

DO

· Do an Internet search for breed-specific rescues and breed clubs, then call them to find out who, in their opinion, is breeding brilliant family dogs of the breed/cross-breed you have chosen. Rescues will have seen it all, from the good to the bad, and the breed clubs will want their breed to keep a good reputation.
· Do talk to the Kennel Club, but be aware that puppy farmers can slip through the net – always be vigilant, even after a recommendation.

- Do go and see lots of litters, as you will start to work out which breeders are doing a better job than others.
- Do question your breeder and they should do the same to you. It should feel like an interview on both sides.
- Do ask for medical information and then talk to your local vet to check that the references and information they have given you is correct.
- Do look for a breeder that is producing dogs for a similar purpose to why you want a dog. For example, if you want a family pet, then you need to find someone breeding for temperament. A show breeder is creating dogs for how they look and a working breeder is creating dogs that can do the job they were designed to do. So you need to find someone who is doing what you need.
- Do sign up to a waiting list if they have one – that is a good sign.

DON'T

- Don't take websites at face value, anyone can market themselves online.
- Don't buy a puppy from a website or social media site. They are totally unregulated and if your puppies are decent you don't need to advertise in this way.
- Don't agree to a breeder dropping the dog off to you, or meeting you halfway.

It's not done out of kindness, it's done because they are running a puppy farm and don't want you to know.
- Don't buy a dog from a shop no matter how beautiful it looks. You simply make way for the next farmed puppy to take its place in the cage – encouraging the trade to continue.
- Don't be taken in by a sob story. If you buy a badly bred puppy you might save that one, but you have just made way for another puppy to take its place – encouraging the abuse. If puppy-farmed puppies or back yard-bred dogs don't sell, there will be no market for them.
- Don't believe any elaborate stories as to why you can't meet the parents. I've heard them all – from the mother being out of the country on a holiday, to at a show, to being on a walk. If you made an appointment to see those puppies, they knew you were coming.
- And also, don't buy a puppy that is living in an environment totally different to what yours will be. If you visit a litter that is living in a garage, removed from the family home and with little access to people, noises and the world, then this dog won't thrive in a city environment. Any dog coming into a family home should be living inside with a family.
- Don't buy a puppy that is too young to be parted from its mother. More on this on page 24.

VISITING THE BREEDERS' HOME

When you have found a breeder and litter you like the sound of, the next step is to visit the breeders' home to meet the mother and, if they own him, the father of the puppies. You should also meet the litter. You can find out a great deal more information this way.

Most importantly, in a good breeders' home I would expect to find a happy, calm, confident and lovely mother of the litter. If the mother is aggressive, anxious, nervous or barking a great deal, I would walk away, as that is an early insight into what the puppies have the potential to be.

When you speak to the breeder on the phone, and when you visit, it should feel like an interview. Any breeder worth their salt will have 101 questions for you. They are trying to find out whether you can offer their puppy the best home possible – if they aren't questioning you, they don't care.

Assuming the puppies are clean, well-cared for, that you like the mother and that you get on with the breeder, there are a few other things you should be looking out for when trying to find your puppy:

· That the dogs are living in the home or at the very least spending big chunks of time indoors. Your puppy needs to be familiar with noises like the radio, the hoover, the washing machine, doorbell and so forth.

· Check out how and where the dogs are fed. If you can't see it, question it. Are they all fed from one big bowl or do they each have their own? Imagine from birth competing for food; I'd bet my house on the fact that a number of the dogs from that litter fed from a shared bowl will have food aggression. Not ideal if you want a family pet and have kids in the house.

· Try to spend some time in the area where the dogs live and play, as you need to look at the resources they have available. Are they in a pen or crate with a lot of different toys and objects, or is there just newspaper on the floor? The more resources available to your puppy from a young age, the less likely they are to guard them in the future, because they never learnt to when tiny. If they have plenty of toys, it also means they are less likely to have been biting other puppies.

· Talk to your breeder about their thoughts on sex and gender differences, it varies greatly between breeds. Asking questions at this point will help you get the right puppy for your lifestyle. It is also worth discussing this with the breed club as they are often people who have worked with the breed for years on end.

WHEN TO TAKE YOUR PUPPY HOME

When you've found your puppy; when you get to the point where you feel like you have found your ideal breeder, that you can trust, that you love her dogs and that you feel they are right for your lifestyle, it's time to decide when to bring your puppy back with you to its new home.

I always recommend that a new puppy is collected in its seventh week (eighth week at the latest). By this point, the pup's mother is packing its bag and pushing it out of the door, and your puppy will be excited about exploring the world – your home. A well-bred puppy should not be coming to you with illnesses, discharges, reactions, feeling poorly or anything of a similar nature. In an ideal situation, your

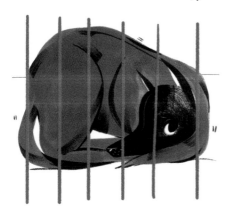

breeder should have given your puppy its first vaccination, microchipped it and given it flea and worm treatments, so that when you get the puppy home you are ready to start your new life together.

FINDING A RESCUE FOR EVER FRIEND

Once you have decided to find a dog that is living in a rehoming centre, you will be as excited as anyone getting a puppy. And just as when looking for a puppy, you cannot underestimate the amount of time searching for your second-hand dog will take.

First, you need to identify the things that are important to you in your search for a dog – is it the breed or is it the personality, are there certain issues you are willing to take on and others that are a no-go area? You have to be honest and upfront with yourself, because when you take a dog home it should be for life, and finding the right dog is as much down to you as it is to the centre that you are visiting.

If you have a particular breed in mind, you can usually find breed-specific rescue groups who are independently run. They will specialise in taking in and rehoming dogs of a certain breed, which means that they will be really well placed to advise you if they have a dog that could suit your situation.

When you first visit a home or approach a breed rescue, you will need to register. The rescue home wants to find the right match for each dog, so the more honest you are, the better. Sometimes it can take a while for your right match to be found – I worked with one client for six months before we found his little Jack Russell, we looked at every shape, size and type of dog under the sun, but now they each have the perfect friend.

Try to remember when visiting a kennel or centre that very often dogs do not exhibit their normal behaviour. Being behind a glass screen or bars, isolated, with little human company, does not make for a really happy dog. So if you see a dog sat at the back of the kennels who doesn't get up and wag its tail each time you pass, do not automatically discount this poor chap. Most kennels are now doing brilliant jobs in trying to provide the best environment they can for their dogs. Try to chat to the kennel staff, the lovely people caring for the dogs on a daily basis, as you may gain some great little nuggets of information.

Most reputable rehoming centres will need you to pass their rehoming process to assess your lifestyle and fit with the dog. A home check should be part of this, and you should visit the dog you are hoping to rehome two to three more times. You need to bring all of the family and any friends/extended family that spend a lot of time at your home.

DOS

· Do make sure that the dog home you are visiting is a registered charity. There are a great deal of well-meaning people setting up rescues with absolutely no idea what they are doing, which may mean you take home a dog that hasn't been tested and assessed.

· Do visit a few homes.

· Do read the 'blurb' on each dog's kennel, but take it with a pinch of salt. The real information is in the dog's file at reception – ask to see it for any dog you are seriously considering. Where possible, you want to find out about the dog's previous situations, why it came in, any problem behaviours identified, any fears or particular things you should be aware of. This is all essential information.

· Do talk to the staff you see working around the centre to find out what they know about the dogs you are considering. They may have info that hasn't yet made it into the file.

· Do go in with an open mind. I have a client who went in looking for a small dog but she came out with a large Rottweiler mix – in terms of personality, the dog was everything she was looking for.

· Do look at the dog's behaviour in the kennel but do not assume that this is normal for the dog. I have seen dogs who look like the devil incarnate behind bars, yet in a real-life situation they are angels. You cannot underestimate the effect of noise, stress, anxiety and hundreds of people walking past you on a daily basis. That said, some dogs' behaviour in kennels is exactly the same outside of them.

· Do take the dog out on a lead where you can spend some time with it. You need to feel a connection with it.

· Do try to find something that the dog enjoys to do when you are taking it out. Does it love to play ball, fetch or sit for a treat? Early on you need to see if there is the potential to form a relationship around things you are happy to do. There is no point taking on a dog obsessed with fetching if you hate this kind of game and want a dog to run with.

DON'TS

· Don't be pushed into a situation, if something doesn't feel right then say 'no'.

· Don't ignore what the rehomers are telling you. Listen to the rescue home's thoughts about children in the home and which dogs they will place with families. There will be a reason for their views, and if you are less than truthful about visiting children or individuals, and if an incident were to happen, the blame can only lie with you.

· Don't fall for the dog with the worst sob story. If a dog has been neglected, abused or worse, it will have very specific requirements and need an experienced owner.

· Don't assume that all second-hand dogs have issues. Often it is a change of circumstances that has resulted in them looking for a home: an owner dying or moving abroad.

· Don't expect to turn up to a centre and walk away with a dog that day. No decent shelter will allow this. If you want this, you need to question your motivations about finding the right dog.

· Don't take short-cuts and look at websites such as second-hand sales' sites. The people selling their dogs in this way do not have the experience and knowledge to assess and test a dog to find it a family.

· Don't waste time when visiting kennels, if you like a dog, get it out and spend time with him. If you really like him, place a reserve on him and get the rest of the family in to meet the rehoming team and organise your home check.

PREPARING FOR ONE OF THE BEST DAYS OF YOUR LIFE

This is it, you finally get to bring your new family member home! There are lots of things you need to think about, and items to buy.

SLEEPING ARRANGEMENTS – CREATING THE 'BED OF JOY'

If you are bringing home a puppy, speak to the breeder about how the dog was raised. If you go too off-piste from what it is used to, you will make life more difficult for yourself. By replicating what the breeder did, you can make the transition far easier. For example, if your puppy is used to a crate or a pen, it should accept this very easily. If your puppy was kept in a utility room with a bed, you could look at doing similar – although most of us in a city don't have the luxury of a separate laundry room!

The aim is to create a space that feels safe and cosy for your dog. If you have taken on a rescue, you may find your dog will favour having their own space in the form of a crate. Each time you visit your dog at the rescue home, try and view him in his kennel. Is he curled up in a ball or stretched out?

This will also help you decide on where your new friend sleeps and what on. Many short-coated dogs like to curl up to keep the heat in, whereas the more lithe dogs like greyhounds quite like to stretch out their long limbs. It sounds strange but

do spend some time looking at this as buying the wrong beds can prove costly, especially if you have taken on a Great Dane where everything needs to be super-sized!

If you have children or visiting children in your home, I favour a crate-type set up. It provides your dog with a safe space for time out, where wandering hands cannot pry and dogs can be left in peace.

Make your dog's bed as comfortable as possible. I call it the 'bed of joy' because your dog should want to sleep in there instead of anywhere else. Most dogs favour a bed with sides that they can lean against and dig into and feel secure in. Pillows and cushions do look beautiful in a living room but generally end up unused as it's actually not that comfy balancing on top of a pouffed-up pillow!

There are some brilliant beds out there:

Tuffies make tough beds for dogs that love to lounge. My favourite is their nest, they are waterproof and, for dogs that love to curl up, they are wonderful.

Bone & Rag make beds that have a raised edge for dogs to rest their heads on and each one comes with a spare cover so you can be washing one while using the other. They also do limited-edition vintage fabrics which are worth keeping an eye out for.

Mungo & Maud their igloo and bolster beds are cosy little dens for puppies and small to medium dogs. All covers are machine washable too.

Cath Kidston has created some fab fabric beds which are lightweight and perfect for the car boot or to travel with.

ChillSpot is an amazing dog bed that keeps your dog cool; it replicates cold tile technology. It's an expensive initial outlay, but if you live in a hot climate and your dog struggles, it is worth the investment.

Speaking from experience, make sure you can throw the bed in the washing machine. Also, as most of us in the city don't have gardens with washing lines to dry and air a vast array of dog blankets, cushions and bedding, you might want to keep things simple.

If you are going to go down the crate route, look online as lots of people are selling them second hand. As soon as you get it home, make sure you give it a good wash and rinse. Put the 'bed of joy' inside and drape a blanket, towel or cover over the back and sides to create a warm environment. Try not to place your dog's bed or crate in a high traffic area like a hallway or entrance to a kitchen, or in doorways or draughty areas. If you take on an elderly dog you can buy heat pads that will keep their older bones warm – or if, like me, you live in an old house with a lot of draughty floorboards, the heat pads can be a welcome addition. Do not put your dog next to a radiator though.

COLLAR, HARNESS, LEAD

There are many different opinions on this subject but one thing for sure is that in public a dog must wear a collar and tag. In the UK, for example, it is a £5,000 fine if your dog is not. In New York, your dog must be licenced and be wearing a tag on their collar with their licence number on it or you can be fined. The purpose of a collar and ID tag is to allow anyone who comes across your dog to be able to return it to you.

If your dog is a puppy, buy nylon collars as within weeks you will be buying new ones. Make sure the collar fits – that it cannot slip over the head but that you can fit two to three fingers (depending on how big your fingers are!) under the collar for the comfort of the dog.

If your dog is older or fully grown, then I advise choosing something like a soft leather collar. One that will age well with time and can be easily wiped clean when it's wet or filthy. If you have a long-haired dog you can find rolled leather collars to save the collar breaking the fur around the neck. Make sure that the hook for attaching the lead is strong and large enough for easy use. In the pouring rain it's not fun trying to fiddle with a tiny loop to get your dog back on the lead – with a wriggly puppy it's like trying to get an eel into a bag! Here are some of my favourite dog collars:

Holly&Lil make beautiful but hard-core collars that do their job brilliantly. I would wait until your dog is fully grown before investing.

Orvis do some great nylon collars which can have your contact details printed directly onto them and are inexpensive. They also do an LED one which is great for night-time walks.

Friendly Dog Collars have created collars that are ideal for dogs that are nervous, fearful or that you are doing training with. They are colour coded and have words such as 'nervous', 'caution', 'friendly', 'deaf', 'blind' etc., printed on them. These collars are invaluable.

Bone & Rag make fabric collars which are a great width for bigger dogs and have large D rings which make clipping the lead on super-easy.

Wonderdog ideal if you want a soft collar decorated with bright fabrics. They can be adjusted to grow with your dog and are easy to throw in the wash if they get filthy.

Harnesses are generally something I try to steer clear of unless you have been specifically advised about them by a trainer and behaviourist. If fitted incorrectly you can end up giving your dog sores. Because of this, most harnesses today are designed to give the dog more ability to pull. Some people buy harnesses because they think it will stop their dog pulling, but if it fastens at the top of the shoulders behind the neck, it won't stop your dog pulling at all – think about how the likes of husky-type dogs are fastened to sledges to pull.

In my view, in a city, one of the worse things ever created is the extendable lead. They are an accident waiting to happen. I once had a dog run around my bare legs in the park and the lead cut straight through my skin. These leads are useless, they never allow your dog to learn to walk on a set length of lead, which is important when treading the streets of a city.

They also mean some lazy owners never teach their dog to recall. And if you have a dog that cannot be off lead for any reason, these are definitely not safe. In a busy city these leads do not have a place, as they give the dog too much freedom and the owner too little control. An alternative is to utilise a training line, which should be used to teach your dog recall and offer you safety and confidence.

My ideal lead is made from soft leather, so it's comfortable to hold with a handle hoop, and at a length where your dog can walk an arm's length away from you. You can also buy some really great leads made out of the material used for horse lead ropes, which are strong and easy to handle. You might like:

Found My Animal create beautiful leads in gorgeous colours made from nautical ropes, that are soft but practical.

They support rescue dogs and each of their leads carry a message for all to see.
Holly&Lil soft leather leads in lush colours, to match Holly&Lil's collars. Best of all, they allow you to decide on the width you would like, which is crucial depending on the size of your dog.
CLIX leads 10m-length training leads which are ideal for teaching your puppy or dog recall while keeping them safe.
Hiro and Wolf have made a hands-free lead which is ideal for walking in the city or running with your dog. You can wrap it across your body, allowing you to keep your hands free to hold bags, push a buggy or find a treat.

FOOD

For the first week of having your new dog in your home, I would feed them whatever the dog was being fed at the breeder's or rescue centre. After this, gradually introduce your own food – flip to the nutrition section of this book on pages 69–75 for some ideas.

Bowls

You will need bowls for your dog to eat and drink out of. There are so many options available now that I would take a look at what suits your dog. If you have a dog with long ears, a Spaniel bowl works brilliantly at keeping those ears dry! If your dog has spent a long time in kennels and become very clever at upturning dishes, then avoid light or metal dishes and go for the heavier ceramic ones. Some lovely bowls include:

Hunter are the best name in metal bowls; durable, easy to travel with and last a long time.

Mason & Cash the original big and chunky ceramic bowls that most dogs cannot pick up or move very easily.

Bone & Rag have got their hands on some very handsome, vintage ceramic bowls. They're beautiful.

Becobowl a lightweight dog bowl made from plant materials. It's biodegradeable and, best of all, not expensive.

Kyjen have created some excellent bowls for fast eaters.

If you are the owner of a larger breed dog, I would recommend investing in a bowl stand. This is basically a platform for the bowls to safely stand on for the dog to eat. The purpose of this is to try to prevent bloat or the gut twisting when the dog eats or drinks. If you are short of space, you can create your own out of a pile of catalogues and milk crates, so that it can be tidied away afterwards. There are also some great slow eating bowls designed for dogs that either eat too fast or need to eat slowly due to their size.

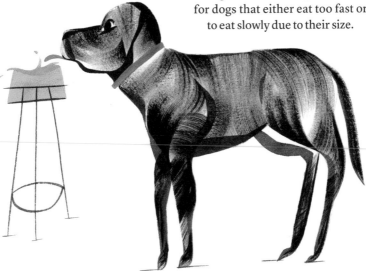

DOG COATS

Dogs wearing coats or jackets is not something I'm usually too keen on, unless your dog really needs it. If you do have one of these dogs, who gets cold and needs an extra layer, there are two great brands doing some brilliant products:

Barbour have created coats which are either padded or waxed to make sure your dog stays warm and dry. They are lightweight, come in practical colours and will last an age, just as their human equivalents do.

Equafleece originally created for horses but now for dogs too. Lightweight and easy to wash, they also keep your dog very cosy. If they get wet, the water sits on top, keeping your dog dry.

DOG GATES

Dog gates are incredibly useful if you live on a busy road, have children, own a cat, are toilet training or you just don't want your dog to have access to a certain room. You can either purchase a run-of-the-mill metal baby gate or you can buy a specific dog gate – these are taller, so that dogs cannot do hurdle practice on them when you aren't looking. Also great for a multi-dog household.

VET

Ideally you will have chosen your vet before bringing your dog home. Your vet will be a friend for your dog's life, and in the next chapter I describe how to find a good one.

BRINGING YOUR DOG HOME

The big day is here! In a perfect world the dog you are transporting home would be placed safely within a crate or the boot of your car with a dog guard firmly fixed. If this is not possible then the alternatives are as follows:

· For a puppy, sit it on your lap on a towel just in case of any accidents.
· For older dogs I would use a car harness if they will accept it. You may need someone to sit in the back seat to supervise.
· If you are unsure how your dog travels then order a dog-friendly cab, or ask a friend to drive, so someone else can focus on the road while you have the dog in the footwell between your legs, on a towel.

· I would avoid public transport if possible, especially for a lengthy journey.

Before you decide when to bring your dog home, it is worth checking whether the dog you like has been car tested. Imagine turning up with your car to bring your new pal home and he's never sat in a vehicle before, you are going to need to prepare for this. If you can, organise to have a friend with a car or a taxi – most taxi services will have dog-friendly drivers, but do call them in good time first to make sure one is available. Car clubs – such as Zipcars in the UK and US, and Flexicars in Australia – are car-sharing schemes where you can hire a car by the hour, which can be perfect for transporting dogs. See pages 123–26 for more tips for travelling with dogs.

2.

HOW TO
CHOOSE A VET

If you are looking for a vet when you have your dog sat by your feet, it's easy to opt simply for the one closest to you. While I understand that in a city it can take time to get across to different areas or districts to see a vet, it really is worth finding someone you can trust. Ideally, you want a vet who has been at their practice for many years, rather than a surgery where there are lots of locums who come and go. You need to build a relationship with someone throughout your dog's life. The best way to find a great vet is to talk to other dog owners and then pay all recommended vets a visit.

Most surgeries are open in the evenings or on a Saturday, so it is easy to book a brief five-minute chat with each vet. You should also like the support staff as they will be your first port of call when making appointments or if you are in a panic about something.

Depending on where you live, most vets are not open 24 hours – there will be emergency practices that they all refer to after hours. Again, take the time to find out the location of where this is, store the phone number and address in your phone – if you are in an emergency situation you will either be getting a cab or driving and will want the address to hand.

It is possible to have a vet come to your home, which I would wholeheartedly recommend if your dog is nervous, has had a bad experience or you are in the terrible situation of having to have your dog put to sleep. Having the vet visit your home means that all treatments can be done where the dog feels the most comfortable – some environments can exacerbate a fear or an issue. Of course, a home visit will be more expensive than visiting a practice. Not all vets offer this service so do ask, otherwise there are specific home vets.

CHIP ON YOUR SHOULDER

Microchipping in the UK will become obligatory by 2016, which is good news. It is already legally required in many Australian states, but is optional in the United States. Wherever you live, ideally your breeder or rescue shelter should put in a chip, or you should do so as soon as you get your dog home. Don't be persuaded to wait until you neuter or vaccinate your dog – a delay could prevent your dog being returned to you if it were stolen, escaped or got scared and ran off. It isn't worth the risk.

Once chipped, be sure you make a note of the chip number in your phone, so that if you ever needed access to it, you have it. It is also key that you keep the details the chip contains – your address and phone number – up to date or you could be liable for a fine. Worse, if your dog ran off the warden might not be able to find you and return your beloved pet. If you move countries, of course, this also needs to be amended.

TO VACCINATE OR NOT VACCINATE

There is a great deal of debate at the moment around the vaccination process in the UK. We have worked hard to keep disease away and this must continue to keep our dogs safe. However there are some new things to potentially consider and it is up to you to take the time to research what you feel suits your dog.

Your dog should be vaccinated at approximately 7–8 weeks and 10–12 weeks, and then your vet may recommend that they have a top-up booster once a year.

The booster is where the controversy lies. Dr Ronald Schultz, Chairman of Pathobiological Sciences at the University of Wisconsin School of Veterinary Medicine, is at the forefront of vaccine research and is one of the world's leading authorities on veterinary vaccines. He believes that the vaccines we are giving dogs provides immunity for up to seven years, which means that we are potentially over-vaccinating our dogs.

To avoid this, an option that is gaining popularity is the titre test. This is a blood test taken by your vet which provides details on your dog's immunity levels. This allows you to decide what, if anything, requires topping up.

A further option is that you don't vaccinate at all, but in my opinion this is very risky – especially living in any city that is densely populated. When you own a dog in the city, you cannot walk out of your home without seeing another hound.

Many veterinarians forbid owners to take their puppies out and about before they have finished their vaccinations at twelve weeks. From a disease control point of view this makes sense, but from a behavioural point of view it spells disaster. In 2011, Battersea Dogs and Cats Home stated that they put to sleep a third of the dogs that they had taken in due to behavioural reasons. It's a sad fact that if you contain your dog, and do not socialise it from the age of six weeks, you will encounter many issues. These could vary from severe to minor but the list is endless: it might be a fear of buses, motorbikes revving, other dogs, children on scooters, men in hats, people in wheelchairs or a particular ethnic group; and living in a city your dog will encounter things, objects, transport, people, animals and equipment on a daily basis.

We need to ensure that our dogs are vaccinated but they are being given the opportunity to get out and about in the big wide world. It is worth discussing this with your vet. I recommend to my clients that they or the breeder do the first vaccination at seven weeks, so that the second can be done at ten weeks. And to make sure the socialisation process starts from day one. I believe in positive and short bursts of exposure to the things that are part of your life, such as public transport, done in a safe and managed way.

NEUTERING

When you live in the city you can meet at least 50 dogs in a week. That is more than 200 dogs a month – a huge number. Your dog will come into contact with some great dogs, and with some not-so-desirable ones. Now, if your dog isn't spayed or neutered, you have more decisions to make.

If you own a bitch (female) dog who hasn't been spayed, she runs the risk of being sought out by the local dogs in town. Male dogs will wander far and wide to find a bitch in season and they can also become aggressive if they have to compete for her.

If you own a dog (male) who hasn't been neutered, then not only do you run the risk of your dog vanishing when he smells a bitch, but you also put your dog at more risk of confrontation with other male dogs. When they are both pulsating with testosterone, there is so much potential for it to kick off. There have also been various reports of people using a bitch in season to lure male dogs and steal them for breeding. It's a hideous thought but it does happen.

The main advantages of neutering your dog are:

· It can reduce unwanted sexual behaviour.

· Male dogs are less likely to mark their territory and pee constantly.

· Male dogs are less likely to stray.

· It can remove the risk of womb infections and various cancers (testicular and mammary).

· It will prevent phantom pregnancies in bitches which can be upsetting and traumatic.

The ideal age to neuter your dog will vary depending on your dog. In the USA it is more common to neuter your puppy at birth, which I totally and utterly disagree with. Some vets will underplay the role hormones can play on a dog, but they are a natural and essential part of a dog's growth. My experience is that if you neuter your puppy too early you can really scupper their development both physically and also in terms of their behaviour.

We should be allowing dogs to reach sexual maturity and then, at the tail end of puppyhood, remove their ability to reproduce. For many, living in the country or less busy areas, neutering might not be a consideration because their dog doesn't come into contact with many other dogs. Which is fine. However when you live in a busy environment, it is worth taking precautions. If your dog ends up with an unplanned pregnancy, the cost of a litter can be around £1,800, and that doesn't even take into account the loss of sleep and the days off of work you will need to take.

For a bitch, I personally like to see them have a first season and then be spayed three months after it has finished – this is the only way to know for sure that a bitch has reached sexual maturity. A season can come as early as six months for some, and nearer twelve months for others – for one it was nearing seventeen months. With a season come hormonal surges; if you allow your bitch to have a first season, wait three months and then neuter. You can generally rest assured that your bitch will have hormonally settled and it's the perfect time to remove their reproductive organs.

With a male dog, I would recommend waiting until he is at least nine to twelve months, where bone development is nearing completion and they are starting to come out of adolescence. Testosterone is also required to allow a male dog to gain confidence and take risks, which means timing is key to prevent creating a nervous and scared dog or a bolshy, over-confident dog. It is a fine balance. Although with some breeds, which mature later, it might be better to wait until they are fully grown – these breeds include the Great Dane, the mastiff, the corgi, the basset hound and the Labrador.

But you want to prevent a problem instead of waiting for one and then neutering. I also strongly feel that it is cruel to keep a dog entire and allow it to walk around your city full of testosterone. You are basically restricting a dog from having sex even though every fibre of its body is telling it to, all because you like to see a huge pair of balls hanging out back as you walk down the street.

In addition, we have far too many dogs in rescue, and neutering programmes can help reduce this. Before you think about having a litter, putting your dog to stud or breeding from your bitch, think about whether it is a wise move. By no means am I against people breeding, it plays a huge role in the future of dogs, but only if it is done well. Much of the time it isn't, and this is the reason for thousands of dogs being put to sleep each year in rescues and stray kennels.

HOW TO RECOGNISE IF YOUR BITCH IS COMING INTO SEASON

For those of you who have no experience of dogs or who have never owned a female, the signs can be hard to spot. One client emailed me in a panic as their dog was due to start a class of mine, saying that she had started bleeding. I gave some advice and then a day later he emailed to say he was wrong; he is a food writer and she had just sat in some beetroot juice!

The first sign of coming into season is that other dogs start becoming very attracted to your dog in the park – sniffing and licking her bottom, and being pretty persistent in this. You will then start to notice that her female genital area becomes swollen and red. This will usually happen before the bleeding actually begins. If your dog is very furry then you may need to have a bit of a pick up and examine! For a first season, the bleeding is usually minimal. It is often more like a brown/red discharge or you may get spotting where she sleeps and on the floor. This is the time you will be thankful for wooden floorboards.

A few of my clients have made use of doggy knickers, which you fasten around your dog's rear end. Most dogs hate them, so only use these if you are desperate. Do not walk your dog in busy areas, allow her off lead or take her to the park when everyone else is walking their dog. I suggest early morning and late evening street walks, as the last thing you want is a harem of males coming from far and wide to seek out your bitch's bottom! A handy thing to carry with you is a big golfing umbrella, so that if a dog does get too amorous you can put it up and around your dog's rear end, protecting her from

his advances. Don't underestimate how quickly a male dog can hop on – once there, the dogs will 'tie' which means they cannot be separated until the deed is done. And then it's too late!

FIRST-AID KIT
FOR DOGS

This is the kind of kit that is worth having to hand, say in the cupboard under the sink, and some bits are worth carrying in the car or in your pockets or dog-walking bag. In the city we are constantly stumbling across random things that can cause problems for our four-legged pals, so being prepared can stop something becoming a bigger issue.

Scissors To cut the fur if something gets caught. Chewing gum is a classic in the concrete jungles.
Sterile eye wash (and dropper) City air is usually the most polluted and come hay-fever seasons it can help relieve itchy pooch eyes.
Tweezers Not just for your eyebrows, great for picking out fragments of glass in paws as you trot past the late-night bar three streets down.

Roll of bandage and tape In case there is a cut or wound, so you can apply pressure, dress it and get your dog to the vet to have it examined.

Antiseptic wipes Brilliant for everything for you, including when you get dog poo on your hand and in your nails and need to get rid before a meeting!

Muzzle Don't be scared of a muzzle, if your dog is in pain they can react by biting. Save both of you the worry, muzzle your dog while you examine if you think they could react badly.

Antibiotic cream or Hydrogel Smother a wound, bite, cut in it and cover up with a clean old sock. Try to avoid your dog licking it all up if you can.

Bach Rescue Remedy drops Useful for after any shock for both you and your dog. I use it in their water bowl, food, onto an open wound and on the tongue.

Phone numbers Have your vet and your local emergency vet numbers in your phone. The last thing you want if there is a problem is to be trying to get online on your phone to find the details.

3.

EXERCISE
AND MENTAL
STIMULATION

EXERCISE

Now, each and every dog is different, but they all need exercise. For many dog owners, their daily walks become unexpected highlights of their day. You get fresh air and exercise yourself, have the best fun with your doggy companion and you really notice the seasons change – something that you can miss living in the city. But living in an urban environment with your dog usually means you need to think a bit harder about how and where you are going to exercise your companion.

Exercise to a dog is vital – it is what makes them happy, satisfied and able to relax, and it provides you with a tired dog that needs to sleep. So you can get on with those emails you need to reply to. Certain dogs need more exercise than others, but on average I would say that all dogs require at least two hours of being out of the house, stimulated, in fresh air and being walked or played with.

When you live in a city, most of the time you can't access acres and acres of fields. We do have some great spaces around us but if you keep visiting the same places over and over, your dog gets bored (and you will too).

There are some easy ways to tell if your dog is bored with you when you are out and about. These vary from barking at you and running away, finding anyone else to play with rather than you. A bored dog will also be hyperactive at home – this can take the form of following you around, nipping, being destructive or just generally being a nuisance.

Exercise is more than your dog following you around on the lead. Their outdoor breaks should include some play, interaction and games with you, sniffing and fun. These games can be anything that your dog enjoys from playing fetch, to hurdling logs, jumping up on benches on command or playing hide and seek.

Many breeders will recommend that you only walk a puppy for five minutes for each month they are old. So if they are five months it would be twenty-five minutes – those of you who have or have owned a puppy will agree that it is a ridiculous recommendation. When you have a dog that is young, they need to learn about the world around them. Twenty-five minutes is barely worth doing. Instead, you need to tailor your exercise regime around your own dog, their ability and their needs.

If you own an active breed or a dog that has a working heritage, you need to invest something more like three hours a day for outdoor exercise. Running or cycling with your dog a few times a week is a great way to bond and also a brilliant way to make the most of the canal paths, the park and cycle routes that encompass the city you live in.

If your dog is under one years old or a large breed (e.g. mastiff, Great Dane, Labrador), then you should try to avoid heavy exertion like jumping or running for long periods as these activities can cause issues when they are older.

In the summer months, if you have access to a safe spot where your dog can swim, it is a brilliant form of exercise. It doesn't place as much pressure on the joints as long as your dog is fit and healthy. Fifteen minutes of swimming is extremely tiring.

Swimming is also a lovely way of your dog cooling down – hot days in the city can be tough on dogs, especially on their feet. The concrete heats up and can in some cases even burn their paw pads. The heat rising off the pavement can be hard to deal with too, especially if you own a breed that is low to the ground.

Conversely, in the winter months, I try to avoid asking dogs to do lots of sits and downs in snowy, cold, damp weather as it's not pleasant for anyone. And if you have a breed that is susceptible to joint problems, avoid getting them wet and damp in cold weather. Although I'm certain my bulldog is part hippo, she loves to wallow in a nice, wet, muddy puddle.

WHAT TO WEAR ON A DOG WALK

As an urban dog walker, we don't trek across mountain plains or spend hours working our way along a beaten track. We can't kid ourselves! Yet we still need a get-up that is practical – and we still want to look good as we walk our dogs to work via the park.

With this in mind I have asked my clients for tips and used my own experiences to come up with some lists that might inspire you. Price ranges vary, but the most common factor for including them is that they provide dry feet, a dry torso, warmth and comfort. My top tip is to avoid walking in flip flops, no matter how hot it is. Dog poo through the toes is never a desirable look, neither is it a pleasure when a dog steps on your bare toe, it hurts. Especially if it's a huge breed with a massive paw!

JACKETS

Where you live and the time of year will inform how much warmth you need, but there is one element to a jacket that every dog walker will find useful: pockets.

Think about the things you need to have with you on a walk – not just your wallet, phone and keys, but also poo bags, treats and a toy or two. That is already about six decent-sized pockets you require. Jackets or coats that are designed for the outdoors are usually best, however some of them can be impractically heavy or expensive. It is always worth searching the likes of eBay for second-hand items, not only are they cheaper, but with wax jackets I find the more battered they are, the more comfortable they are too. My best springtime jacket is a family hand-me-down of a Burberry wax jacket. It is over 30 years old and it is lovely and worn, super-comfy and has pockets galore.

These are the brands that came up as doing an all-round sterling job:

Barbour classic British outdoor wear who have a genius jacket called 'The Beagle' designed to be worn on dog walks. It has lots of pockets and finishes below the waist, making bending to pick up tennis balls nice and easy.

Carhartt a NYC brand that does lots of lightweight jackets brilliant for those who hate heavy coats, and their colours are fairly neutral.

Canada Goose as the name suggests, made in Canada for the hardcore and those who hate the cold. It's like wearing a duvet on a walk. Just bear in mind that wet down is not pleasant, so I prefer these for cold but not wet days.

Uniqlo Japanese brand doing some brilliant high-street-priced jackets that are warm and come in great colours.

WELLIES

Now these are a staple in every dog walkers' wardrobe, often worn come rain or shine. But when you walk in the city, you aren't just on soft terrain. You are walking through concrete streets littered with remnants that can pierce and destroy a rubber boot. If you are concerned with mud more than paddling, it is worth

looking at proper walking boots as they are often more sturdy. But many manufacturers have upped their game and are producing some wellies that can really do the job. It is definitely worth saving up and spending a bit more if you can, as you will reap the benefits – not only in comfort but also in the length of time they last. You can also now find wellies which come fleece or sheepskin lined, which can seriously make all the difference when it is bitterly cold outside.

Barbour good old-fashioned English wellington boots that are reasonably priced and do a great job. This brand has managed to move with the times without forgetting the reason they were originally invented.

Redwings a brilliant US boot that looks good and gets the job done. They can take a bit of wearing to get them to the point where you find them comfortable. Once done, though, they last an age.

Nokian a Norwegian boot that is definitely very sturdy, and Julia Lundsten has created some excellent designs that make wearing wellies in the city not seem silly. They do a cropped biker boot version which is ideal for wearing with jeans.

Dr. Martens a British boot that moves from walk to work wear very easily. They have an air-cushioned sole so for days when I'm out for long periods, they really do stay comfortable.

TOPS

Crucial to keep the draughts out. You want them warm, cosy and covering the back as there is nothing worse than bending to collect the dog poo and your back being exposed and cold. But also because many of my clients walk their dogs before work, or on the way, they need to be smart enough for the office. Avoid man-made, cheap fibres as they shrink and make you sweat. Layering tops is a good way of keeping warm.

American Apparel a rainbow of coloured hoodies that look great with anything.

Uniqlo HeatTech thermals – cosy, soft Japanese fabrics that you can layer.

Boden a British brand but with some affordable wool-mix jumpers and some great cashmere ones that really do create a wind block under your coat when you are out and about. Plus they come in the brightest of colours.

SEASONS IN THE CITY

It's worth bearing in mind how the passing seasons can take their toll on your dog – a little preparation can make yours and your dog's life easier.

WINTER

Your winter might be a mild 10°C (50°F) or several degrees below zero, but it's always the coldest time of year with the most 'interesting' weather. Here are my top tips:

· If your dog is shorthaired or delicate then it will need a coat. If your dog has a lot of hair and likes the mud, wind and rain then leave him to his own devices.

Some dog clothing goes too far. I am not a fan of dog coats with hoods, they are quite frankly useless. And I often see owners who wrap their cockapoos up in waterproof coats that cover their entire body – I understand the attraction but I don't understand why anyone would choose a hairy, dirty dog in the first place if they mind hair and dirt all over their house. Even in winter, your dog needs to be a dog.

· Leave a damp towel by your front door so you can wipe and remove the mud on entering the house. In winter I also put a few drops of essential oil like lavender on the towel to get rid of the dirty smell.

· When it is really cold and the pavements are frozen, packed with snow or soaking wet, don't be surprised if your dog refuses to do a sit.

· Always be aware of puddles near parked cars, as any type of antifreeze can be lethal to an animal – do not let your dog drink from puddles that have a glaze or look coloured in the sunlight.

· If you have a dog with lots of hair, I advise getting their paws trimmed ahead of the cold weather to stop mud or snow matting causing issues. Ask your groomer to trim the under paw, around the claw and dew claw.

· It is also worth remembering that from November, many people will use fireworks for celebrations such as Bonfire

Night, Thanksgiving, Christmas and Chinese New Year. Kids will also buy them and let them off at any time of day, so be super-vigilant and look out for discarded remnants on the street and in the park.

· There are also a few plants that appear around Christmas which can be toxic to your dog if ingested. These include holly berries, mistletoe berries, and the leaves, stem and flowers of the poinsettia plant, and even your pine tree.

SPRING

Usually this is a delightful time of year for a dog, because it's cool outside but the ground isn't too boggy – it makes chasing after that ball even more fun.

· The flowers and trees are starting to bloom so it is worth having an idea of some of the plants that are dangerous for your dog to munch on. There is a huge list but some of the most common are the following: bluebells, buttercups, cyclamen, daffodil bulbs, foxglove and hyacinth and tulip bulbs. If you are in any doubt of how much your dog has consumed then speak to your vet immediately.

· Spring showers can catch you out, so get a light raincoat and be prepared to seek shelter in a sudden downpour!

SUMMER

A joyful season for many humans but harder for most dogs, as the heat can make exercising more of a chore.

· I advise early morning and late evening exercise. Try to avoid going out in the hottest hours of the day as your dog cannot sweat as you are able to. Their systems for cooling down are just panting and sweating through their paws, and if you are walking your dog on a hot pathway, it's going to make this extremely difficult to do. Being left at home in a well-ventilated, cold-floored area is preferable to forcing your dog to accompany you to the cafe in the midday heat.

· If you can, find somewhere safe for your dog to swim. If they need encouragement, try throwing them a floating toy on a rope or long line and asking them to fetch at greater and greater distances.

· If you don't have much water near you then it's worth investing in a kid's paddling pool or a big plastic bowl that your dog can get in, drink from and play in. They are also really easy to use when you only have a balcony, roof terrace or small yard. You can put in floating treats for them to jump in and retrieve, or if your dog adores ball games then encourage them to play with a few balls in the water.

· Another really easy way to cool your dog down is to teach them to drink from one of the plastic plant sprayers. I fill mine up with water, place it in the freezer so the water goes ice cold and then use it to spritz dogs on the chest, belly and ears and then allow them to drink from it. It is a practical way to keep your dog hydrated if you do have to take them out for any reason.

· Try to avoid taking your dog on public transport. Often their ventilation systems are not sufficient to keep your dog cool.

· If you don't have air con, a cheap fan is a brilliant investment. If you are out for a few hours, leave it on and know your dog is nice and cool. Do remember to shut blinds and curtains to keep the heat out and create a shaded area.

· It you have a doggy door, make sure it's closed when you aren't home – not only for security, but also because if your dog decides to go outside and sunbathe unsupervised, he could end up with serious sun stroke. Sun stroke can take hold really quickly and it is extremely dangerous.

· Always make sure your dog has access to fresh water.

AUTUMN

If your dog is a natural forager, then this will be their favourite time of the year. The leaves are falling, the ground is damp and it is the perfect time for your dog to snuffle around in. It is also the hardest time of year to pick up dog poo as it seems to blend in perfectly with the mud and leaves laying on the floor! So keep your eyes peeled and ready to pounce with that poo bag.

· If the wind starts blowing it can really disorientate your dog – it blows all the scents from other areas into the location where you are walking. Some dogs who are really very sensitive to scent or noise can be quite freaked out by such weather. If your dog is one of these or you aren't yet sure, keep them on a lead or long line to ensure their safety.

MENTAL STIMULATION

This is the dog version of checking emails, reading, doing a crossword or playing Scrabble – basically, putting their mind to work. If you can incorporate this into their daily or weekly lives your dog will be so much more happy. Keep them entertained and they will be your No.1 fan, which in honesty is what we all want – for our dog to think that we rock their world because we are just so wonderful.

Mental stimulation can take many shapes and forms, it is all about working out what makes your dog tick. Is it the movement, the tearing about, the food, the challenge, or it may be all of the above? With any of these ideas, start gently and show your dog what to do. They don't automatically know what you are expecting them to do, so teach them. Slowly but surely their confidence will soar and so will your love of having a calm dog. The key is making sure that the toy you are creating motivates them – if it doesn't your dog will sit in front of you and just stare you out. So here are some ideas to get you started. They have all been tried and tested on hundreds of dogs all over the world, so I know they work, just try them out to see what suits you and

your dog and life. I've also put a line under each on how to make it trickier, the quicker and cleverer they get.

These ideas are designed to be used in collaboration with physical exercise, so that when you are in the house/garden/balcony/office you can entertain your dog and it also learns to do things independently. They are a good way to teach a puppy or dependent rescue dog that their world is great even when you aren't actively playing a role in it. Brilliant to teach a dog some confidence and to succeed at a task, especially if you have a nervous dog that needs a boost. Just select the right toy and let it take its time.

DOGGY PIÑATA

Take an old tennis ball that your dog has broken, as in it doesn't bounce any more. Cut a hole in one side, big enough that treats can get in and out. Load it up with tasty morsels and let your dog at the treat-dispensing ball.

Next level: to make it trickier, tie fabric around the ball so that the fabric has to be removed before they can get treats out.

JUICY JOY

Using an old, clean juice carton, cut out the plastic pouring piece at the top and leave a hole. Now fill it with either one of your dog's meals or smelly treats. Let them tear it to bits.

Next level: fill it up and then hide it inside another box which you seal so they have to tear open two layers to reach the treats inside.

PASS THE PARCEL

Take a big, smelly treat that your dog loves, e.g. rawhide, a raw bone, marrow bone, etc. Place it in a box and seal it shut but poke some holes in the sides. Wrap it up in paper and then tie string/rope around the box like a gift. And present it to your dog!

Next level: hide the box in the room for them to seek it out before they can destroy it all.

MUFFIN MADNESS

You need a muffin tray that you use to bake cakes in the oven, they usually have twelve holes in them. Fill each hole with a treat. Cover each treat with a different item, such as a ball, a rope, a toy, a cup etc. Let your dog work out how to pick up each item to remove the treat.

Next level: put the treats in every other hole so that they have to sniff each individual one.

PLASTIC FANTASTIC

Find a big yoghurt-pot-shaped container which your dog cannot snap or break. Fill it up with wet food, raw food, cheese spread, peanut butter, or even make layers if you fancy. Now compact it very tightly and let your dog lick it all out. The tub should be small enough that they can get their tongue in and snout but not small enough that they can try and get it all in their mouth to chew it up.

Next level: freeze it! This makes it really tricky and very time-consuming for your pet.

ROLL-UP, ROLL-UP

This is a great trick for when you are desperate and have nothing with you but you are on the bus or sat in a really busy area and need your dog to focus. Simply hide a treat in the roll-up of your trouser leg near your shoe. Let your dog sniff, scuffle and dig their way to get it out. Once they have discovered it, ask them to sit or do a down and get the treat out for them.

It certainly isn't a game I'd encourage frequently, but desperate times call for desperate measures. Hopefully not too many passers-by will be aware of what's going on!

4.

DOG WALKER OR DOGGY DAY-CARE?

Ideally you will be around to spend time with your dog during the day. But for those occasions when you're not, you may be considering whether to use doggy day-care or having a dog walker.

In recent years there has been a surge of people setting up both businesses. They can be very lucrative, so I can see why. However, when it comes to your dog, you don't want money to be their carer's key motivation.

DAY-CARE

Doggy day-care started in the USA and there are some places doing it brilliantly. However, many leave a great deal to be desired. I have experienced day-care that is basically a holding station for dogs who are then taken out for a dog walk twice a day. All of their time is spent in the company of dogs with very little human contact, which will lead to behavioural issues. If dogs are allowed constant access to each other, to play and to rough and tumble non-stop, it can create a dog which becomes fixated on other dogs rather than prioritising humans. This is problematic – a point in hand, a young dog is in a day-care or goes out with a dog walker who encourages constant rough housing with the other dogs. This young dog starts to bolt when it sees dogs in the park, running straight up to them to instigate the play he has become accustomed to. One day he runs into the wrong dog and gets told off or attacked, this happens twice more over the course of a month. Now the young dog, who is a bit older, starts running into other dogs but barking and ready to attack instead of to play. Do you see how the path of events in a dog's daily life can impact on their behaviour by their experiences and associations? This dog started off with good intentions, but through three experiences of being attacked, paired with his carers teaching him a focus on dogs is acceptable, he started to put the wrong things together. He learnt that to go on the defensive and be aggressive, and to charge a dog, is the best course of action. We have now created an aggressive dog that will actively seek out another dog to start on. Obviously not all cases are like this, but it illustrates just how much you need to consider what your dog is doing on a daily basis.

If you are considering day-care, go and visit, and ask lots of questions. Look at what the standard accommodation is for your dog – is it as comfortable and interesting as your own home? Will they be mixing with other dogs continually, or do they have their own time-out space?

What is the exercise provision? How many dogs are taken out at one time, and where to? Who are the people working with your dog? What is their background, where do they come from and why are they working with dogs? For many it's a pit stop, a bit like waitressing, while they try and do other things. This is fine, as long as their heart and soul is in it – your dog is precious to you so the people taking care of it should be doing a great job when you aren't able to.

An advantage of day-care is that many will pick up and drop off your dog, but make sure you inspect the vehicle. Is it adequately decked out for the cold winter months and the hot summer months? Ask how long your dog will be in the vehicle – it can be as much as three hours a day. Can the driver see and hear the dogs? If not, how do they monitor if the dogs are happy and safe?

Lastly, after you've left, think carefully about whether the day-care centre will cause more problems than it solves. It's not that I'm adverse to day-care. It can be a great way to entertain a dog a couple of days a week when you can't, but if it's done badly — well, I've seen some of the side-effects first hand. Take the time to do your research until you find somewhere you are totally happy with and where you can see your dog enjoying himself without you.

DOG WALKERS

Personally, I suggest that every single dog owner has a dog walker. I'm not saying to use one every day, but it is beyond great to have a trusted walker who has keys to your home who can help you out when you are in a tight pickle, on deadline or feeling ill. In general, no dog should be left alone for more than four hours at a time. If you need to leave them, try to get a walker in to collect your dog at this interval to break up their day.

A dog walker ideally should be someone who is doing the job because they love it, not because they worked out that walking fifteen dogs in one go earns them the most cash. Try to find someone who comes recommended and who you really like. As well as looking after your precious dog, they are going to have access to your home when you aren't there, so you need to trust them. Ideally they would do sole dog walks or take out no more than three dogs at a time, so they can keep an eye on what your dog is getting up to. If you have a young dog, you will need to know about its toileting habits and so on. If you have a rescue dog, I would look at sole dog-walking sessions while you work out the lie of the land and your priorities.

When you take a dog walker on, pay for the walker to come on a couple of walks with you. You can show them what you do, how you do it and what your dog loves or dislikes. This is the benefit of having someone just one-to-one with your dog.

QUESTIONS FOR ANY POTENTIAL CARER

You should also be questioning the walker or day-care about their ethos of working with dogs. Walk away immediately if they believe that dominating a dog is key to 'making them learn'. You need to be 100 per cent certain that this person has the same ideas as you do, otherwise problems will certainly arise. If in doubt, hang around the parks and observe the person/s you are thinking of taking on. Are you happy with the way the dogs are handled, released from the van, walked, communicated with? If you aren't happy with what is being done with other people's dogs, you won't be happy when it is your hound.

Walkers and day-care must be insured to walk your dog – always ask to see their insurance paperwork.

The city is a big place and it's important you spend the time to find someone who is the perfect fit for you and your dog. You are paying them, so they should be providing the service you have agreed on.

A great dog carer should:

· Be insured.
· Leave you a note, text or email you an update after each session.
· Know about your dog and what it loves to do.
· Be trustworthy, they should turn up on time and do the amount of time agreed.
· Know who your vet is and have their contact details.
· Be kind and don't use any corrective, or punishment-type techniques.

FIVE WAYS YOU KNOW YOU ARE
OBSESSED WITH YOUR DOG

———

1. YOU SET UP A TWITTER/INSTAGRAM/BLOG FOR YOUR DOG.

2. YOU STOP TAKING HOLIDAYS ABROAD, NOT BECAUSE OF THE CARBON FOOTPRINT BUT BECAUSE YOUR DOG CAN'T GO WITH YOU!

3. YOU PREFER TO SHARE YOUR BED WITH YOUR DOG THAN YOUR PARTNER.

4. YOU SKYPE YOUR DOG WHEN YOU ARE AWAY WITH WORK.

5. YOU DRESS IN MATCHING SWEATERS IN THE LEAD UP TO CHRISTMAS.

5.

WHAT TO FEED YOUR BELOVED DOG

There are always passing fads and trends in food, and this includes dog food and treats. But the make-up of a dog has never changed, they are a carnivore species designed to eat meat, vegetables and fruit. Try to feed your dog as close to real food as possible. This means real ingredients that you recognise.

From a training and behavioural point of view, the food you put into your dog can have a huge effect. If you feed them highly processed, nutritionally depleted food, your dog may be hyperactive, have poor focus, be hungry all the time, like to scavenge and may even seek out the likes of cat faeces. It's like saying that feeding your child sweeties and chocolate for breakfast and supper is ideal. We all know that isn't the case.

Also bear in mind that one food most certainly does not fit all. Your dog's diet should also be tailored around *your* dog. A rescue dog, for instance, will have different requirements to a puppy. Owners often take advice on feeding their dog from their vet, which in general would make sense. But vets are not always an independent source of information – many will have particular brands for sale in their surgery, which suggests that their advice may not always be impartial. They may even be receiving commission for each product they sell you. Instead, unless you have come across a holistic vet, I recommend you speak to an independent canine nutritionist. I have done this for my dog Cookie for six years, after she developed red hot spots on her face and body and would often refuse food.

For this book I have spoken to nutritionist Alison Daniels to give you the best advice possible. We both advocate a natural diet which can be raw or cooked, and which you can buy or you can make yourself, depending on your lifestyle.

COOK IT YOURSELF

Cooking food can remove nutrients, but it's a very practical way to feed your dog. You can easily create meals in bulk for your dog using cheap but good-quality ingredients. Think of it like cooking for a baby, no seasoning and no preservatives, sugar or salt should be added to the food. Keep it as simple as possible – you are making a bland casserole with a protein (e.g. fish, meat, poultry), vegetables, fruit and a small amount of carbohydrate. A nutritionist can also advise on adding supplements such as bone meal, salmon oil, flaxseed and so forth.

RAW FOOD

Your dog's stomach is designed to eat meat and eating it raw is perfect for most dogs. You are feeding the purest form of a meal in this way, with the simplest ingredient. The raw diet was introduced by an Australian vet called Dr Ian Billinghurst whose book, *Give Your Dog A Bone,* is incredibly informative and well worth reading. One of the biggest myths that surrounds raw food is that it is dangerous. In truth, it is only a problem if you are using poor-quality meat or not feeding it fresh. All meat should be fit for human consumption and certainly not a by-product that is too gruesome for a human to eat. It should be kept in airtight Tupperware containers and defrosted fully from the freezer before feeding.

Bones can be great if fed properly. In a city we do not have the time, inclination or – most importantly – access to start catching our own meat to feed our dogs. (A city dog would not thrive on rat, squirrel or pigeon.) As a general rule of thumb, try to avoid cooked bones and any small bones that can snap or splinter or be swallowed whole.

If in doubt, purchase a food product where the raw food is created for you and the bone, meat and veg is ground up into a container and frozen for you to defrost and serve. Do look at making sure the food suits your dog and their output. Working dog type foods are usually only suitable for highly active working dogs.

TINS

People find tinned food for dogs confusing. Only consider tins if they contain real ingredients. If they hold hideous ingredients such as chicken meal (meat not fit for human consumption, and can be preserved with antifreeze like chemical Ethoxyquin, which doesn't have to be on the label), wheat flour (the lead cause of allergies in dogs), beet pulp (sugar), maize (a filler), or animal by-products or derivatives, then step away from the shelf. Many brands use jelly as a binder and cheap filler and the chunks of meat are so far away from being meat, it's astonishing. The food shouldn't smell. If you open a can of food and it smells unpleasant, what on earth will it do to your dog's insides?

If you see 'organic' on the packaging, it's one of the only ways to know that the food is as pure as it can be, that nothing has been added and that the real items listed on the tin or pack.

DEHYDRATED

You can now buy dehydrated natural food, which when rehydrated means the food retains 90 per cent of its nutrients. To make them up it's usually a cup of the food mixed with the same amount of hot water to rehydrate the food. This is wonderful news for when you are travelling or don't have time to prepare anything – use them as a base, and you can add your own scraps to it as needs be. If you take your dog to work and need to keep some emergency supplies, this is a great option.

DRIED FOOD

As a general rule of thumb, I advise clients to not feed a dry food or kibble. I cannot under any circumstances see how anyone can tell an owner that a bag of dry kibble is the same as or better than a bowl of cooked chicken, rice, carrot, peas and broccoli! Most of a bowl of kibble just comes out the tail end of the dog. Dogs do not digest rice, pasta, soya or wheat well. An experiment if you currently use dried food: look at the quantity you are feeding in the bowl and then look at the quantity coming out the other end. Your dog should using what it is eating, if they aren't it will just be passing through until it meets your poo bag!

TOP TIPS

There are some key things to think about when feeding your dog a natural diet:

· Raw bones, rawhide and vegetables can be nature's toothbrush, you do not need weird chemical pastes with artificial chicken to brush your dog's teeth. A big, chunky raw bone like marrow bone will do the job brilliantly – it will also exhaust your dog! Just never leave your dog unsupervised.

· Try to vary the protein you are feeding your dog, variety is the joy of a dog's diet. I also find it can help stop a dog scavenging if they are having their needs met at home.

· Poultry can be the protein that dogs will have the most reactions to, it is one of the most farmed and overused.

· Buy the best-quality food you can afford and, where possible, buy organic when it comes to the likes of liver and heart.

· Add scraps into your dog's bowl from the family meal – as long as it's not processed or heavily seasoned.

· In terms of quantity, there is no right or wrong amount. Feed more on a day that you dog has done more and less when it hasn't. If your dog puts on weight, decrease the amount. Go with your instincts.

· Avoid anything heavily processed, sugary, salty and man-made.

· Tripe is a great mixer for dogs but some can find it too rich, so don't give too much in one go.

· You do not have to feed your dog something exclusively, you can mix and match to suit your life and your dog's tastes. One of the key things in the feeding stakes is understanding your dog because each dog is different, in the same way that we are.

FOODS FOR HEALTH PROBLEMS

Differing experiences can also affect your dog's nutritional needs.

· A puppy will require more protein for bone development up until around six months old.

· A rescue dog that has been in a kennel environment may be Vitamin C deficient due to stress.

· A dog who has been put on an antibiotic course may require immunity support and probiotics.

· An older dog may need specific nutrients added to its diet.

As well as making the most of Western medicine, a nutritionist can help you look at nature's pantry to help with all of these situations. What you feed your dog can have a great impact on your dog's future. Below are a few examples of some natural products that you can utilise for your dog:

Honey a natural antibacterial.
Natural yoghurt a probiotic.
Tinned fish in oil omega oils for skin, ears and eyes (there are risks with mercury and fish so should not be fed daily).
Coconut oil antibacterial, antiviral and antifungal. One of my favourite items ever.
Spinach natural cleanser.
Neem leaf anti-fungal.
Flaxseed for digestion.
Sweet potato full of fibre.

TOXIC FOODS

There are also a few foods that can be toxic to some dogs. These are:

· Chocolate
· Grapes
· Raisins
· Onion
· Avocado

RECISE

LIVER CAKE

A high-value treat used to train your dog to do something quite tricky or that they find hard.

450 g (1 lb) chicken or lambs liver (try to use organic where possible)
2 garlic cloves
3 eggs
milk
450 g (l lb) self-raising flour

1. Blend the raw liver up with the garlic to liquid consistency.
2. Beat the eggs separately, then add to the mixed eggs a matching quantity of milk.
3. Mix the two together in a bowl and slowly add the flour.
4. Once thoroughly mixed, put into a baking tray. If you have any veg or meat scraps in the fridge throw these in too.
5. Bake for 35–40 minutes on 180 °C (350 °F/gas mark 4).
6. Put a knife into the tray, if it comes out clean they are ready.
7. Leave to cool and then cut into mouth-sized pieces.

Because this is made from fresh ingredients, it will go off within a couple of days, so keep a handful out and then separate the rest into little bags to freeze. Defrost as required.

RECOVERY RECIPE

Great for a dog that is in recovery from illness, the coconut oil in this recipe is anti-bacterial, anti-fungal, anti-viral – and tastes delicious!

2 teaspoons of coconut oil
250 g (6 oz) lean beef mince (change the protein to suit your dog)
250 g (6 oz) cooked brown wholegrain rice
handful of chopped spinach

1. Heat the coconut oil in a pan, as soon as it turns liquid add in the mince.
2. Once browned add in the rice and spinach and heat through.
3. Let it cool and serve, little and often, to a convalescent dog.

You can refrigerate or freeze the leftovers and serve as needed, hot or cold.

FROZEN FRUIT SALAD

This is so easy but perfect for hot days.

Cut up into generous bite-sized wedges of fruits like mango, pineapple, banana and oranges. Pop them onto a plate and freeze. Once cold and icy serve them individually to your dog as a cool-down treat or as a fruit salad if they are sunbathing!

SWEET POTATO CHEWS

Full of fibre, super-easy and you can eat them too. Great for dogs that love to chew.

Buy the longest sweet potato you can find and give it a wash. Pat it dry and then cut lengthways into thin strips, so they are long, wide yet thin. Preheat the oven to 180°C (350°F/gas mark 4). Pop the strips on a baking tray and bake for 3 hours. Let them cool and store in a container.

BANANA POT

1 banana
1 small pot of plain, natural, probiotic
    yoghurt
runny honey

Blend all of the ingredients together until they are smooth and can be poured. Pour into the empty yoghurt container and freeze. Once frozen, cut the pot off and give it to your dog in hot weather or if teething. Ideally, do this outside as it can get messy.

6.

THE ANATOMY
OF A DOG

If you know how your dog experiences these vast cities we live in, it will help you to understand both his behaviour and some of his preferences in life.

NOSE

A dog's nose is how your dog sees and interprets the world. Every time you see its snout moving, foraging, vacuuming in the air or just holding it high while it takes in a waft of scent, it's similar to when you read something. Dogs use scent as a way of understanding what they are encountering. On a dog walk, you'll notice some scents seem to take longer to 'read' than others, that's because some are much more complicated.

The smell of something has a huge impact on a dog's reactions. One of the reasons why a dog can be scared of fireworks is the smell of the gunpowder and the burnt scent that accompanies the bangs, flashes and high-pitched squeals. It is also why many dogs are used for medical detection, or to sniff out drugs at the airport, or to find land mines in the ground. Their scent receptors are the key to doing their job. Of all the senses for a dog to lose, this would be the worst. And when a dog goes deaf or blind, it's their sense of smell that usually heightens. It is certainly true in the case of my bulldog who went deaf three years ago.

To give you an idea of just how different we are when it comes to smell:

Nose scent-detecting cells (approx.)

Human	5 million
Dachshund	125 million
Beagle	225 million

Astounding, isn't it! So when your dog turns its nose up at something, rest assured it knows something you don't. It is also why dogs can suffer from hay fever. Their noses are so sensitive that the same things that trigger hay fever reactions in humans can do the same to our four-legged friends.

Another amazing fact: your dog's nose-print is totally individual to your dog, the same as your fingerprints are to you.

EYES

Owners often get confused why their dogs cannot see something they have thrown. To you it might look obvious, but your dog doesn't have a clue. One reason is that their nose is their primary sense, but also it's because dogs see everything in shades of blue and yellow. It is why dogs can find it so hard to see a yellow tennis ball in green grass. Dogs see orange, yellow and green as similar light shades, so if you want to help them out use a ball that is a dark shade – red or black – so it stands out.

Sights of the city humans of every ethnicity, vehicles speeding past, miles of pavement, children and buggies, market stalls, dogs on every corner, squirrels scrambling up trees.

EARS

The type of ear your dog has can affect their hearing. For example, dogs with pricked up, open ears are far more likely to be reactive to sounds than the long, floppy, closed ear-dogs. The open ears are also able to move round, to try to locate the sound that they can hear – it's why you can see dogs doing the cocked head position with moving ears if you make a strange noise to them. It takes about 18 muscles for your dog to move its ears in this way.

It is thought that the average dog can hear four times the distance of the average human.

Sounds of the city sirens, bus air brakes, shouting at 3 a.m. when night revellers return home, Tannoy announcements on the train, constant noise.

TEETH AND MOUTH

Puppies will usually begin teething from around four weeks old, and adult dogs should end up with a full set of 42 teeth.

Due to the dry kibble (and some brands of tinned food) of many dog's diets being stuffed with the likes of sugar and salt, our dogs can suffer from some really horrible dental problems such as cavities, plaque and severe decay. These can create massive health implications for the rest of their bodies: a dog's diet should not include sugar, salt, flavourings or preservatives (see What to feed your beloved dog, pages 69–75).

If you have an adult dog it's a good idea to discuss dental hygiene with your vet.

Poison on our city streets

Human faeces and vomit hidden in park bushes are sadly usually highly attractive to dogs – they can also be laced with drugs and alcohol. Also be aware of pest control pellets for rats.

A bite pressure study was carried out by *National Geographic* to gauge the strength of various animals if they bite. I think it's really interesting.

Pounds of bite pressure

Human	120 pounds
Dog	320 pounds
Lion	600 pounds
White shark	600 pounds

Taste of the city the streets become an urban delicatessen, with discarded chicken carcasses, dropped sweets, cigarette ends and leftover kebabs.

FUR

The majority of dogs are covered in fur, which is designed to protect them from the likes of scratches, bites, cuts and from the weather. Your dog's coat is also an indication of what job their breed was used for in the past.

A Border terrier is double-coated to keep out the rain as they originate from the borders of Scotland. Used for hunting out small rodents, their coat needed to protect them but be smooth enough not to hinder them or get in the way.

A Border collie is designed to herd and be outdoors for hours on end, so a long, warm coat is required without reducing their speed.

A poodle was used in hunting as a water-retrieving dog – the tight, curly coat kept them warm and stopped water from penetrating when working outdoors.

The feel of the city broken glass can litter the streets, dog poo gets left and walked through, people will try to touch your dog and the pavements can be tough places to walk on continuously.

TAIL

We all love to see our dog wagging their tail when we come through the door, it has to be one of the best things ever. The tail's main purpose is for balance. When you see a dog swimming, such as a Labrador, their tail becomes their propeller and their rudder. It really is a clever thing!

A tail can be sprained and, worst of all, broken, and this is why that some working breeders still dock their litter's tails. It is now illegal in the UK unless you can prove the dog is required for working purposes. The docking process is unnecessary and can be detrimental to the dog – especially when you look at how expressive a tail is for communication purposes.

Do not always assume that a wagging tail is a happy tail. Dogs wag their tails like we breathe – they have no control over it. So a dog going into a fight, or a dog that is scared, will still move its tail but in an entirely different fashion (see Tail Positions on page 110 for more on this).

The tail is also an excellent wafter, all the movement really helps propel the scent from their anal glands. When you see a dog tucking its tail between its legs and moving away, it's the dog equivalent of trying to make yourself disappear.

ANAL GLANDS

A pleasant one to end on! All dogs have them, but some cause more issues than others, and they are often a topic that doesn't get discussed. The anal glands sit either side of the anus and when a dog poos, the glands coat it in a scent. This is healthy and means the glands get emptied regularly.

Problems occur when the glands don't empty and get impacted or blocked. If your dog drags its bottom across the carpet, this is most likely why – it creates some friction! Many dogs who are fed a bland, dry diet will suffer from gland issues, as the food does not produce hard, firm stools that help the glands empty. Soft poos are not good for the anal glands. They're not good for picking up or for the nose, either!

The way to know if your dog needs some help is usually one of two ways, the first is the dragging of the bottom and the second is the rather putrid fishy smell that will be lurking around their rear end. Believe me, when you smell it you know it.

Some dogs, if they are absolutely petrified, will empty their glands as the body's reaction to stress. This often happens with stray dogs in kennels.

7.

PUPPY TRAINING

Toilet training is one of the main reasons why young dogs get given up. New owners cannot believe just how hard it is to do.

The key things to remember are:

· Generally a puppy, unless your breeder has done the work for you, will have no idea where you want them to toilet when you first bring them home.
· Your dog does not speak English.
· Puppy pads hinder toilet training.
· Your aim is to teach your dog that inside is toilet free and outdoors is toilet galore.
· When your puppy is very young its brain and its bladder/bowels do not seem to be connected.

Set you and your puppy up for success. You need low-level (not very exciting but edible) treats and a designated space where you want your dog to go. In the city it might be a balcony, a roof terrace, a garden or on the street. Wherever it is that works for you is fine, as long as it is safe, secure and your puppy isn't going to get scared.

Look at the breeder's set-up before you leave their home. Find out how far the puppy has progressed and what they have and haven't been allowed to do. If the breeder has been teaching the dogs to pee on paper inside the house, your dog will be looking for similar in your home. If they have had access to just grass then you may find your dog resistant to concrete. All of these early experiences have a great deal of influence on your new dog and doing this background research will equip you well.

If you have taken on a rescue dog, discuss it with the kennel staff. They will be able to tell you how your dog was doing in the kennel environment. Many rescue dogs will struggle with toilet training, especially overnight as they are left for long periods locked inside. Once they are home and given the chance to go outside and in again, they will happily go back to only toileting outside.

When trying to teach your dog where and when to go the toilet, you need to try and put these key things into place.

IN THE HOME

· Keep your dog with you or in your sight. Do not allow your dog to go wandering, as that is when accidents behind the potted plants happen. An undiscovered dog poo does not make a great home scent!
· If you need to leave your dog or get in the shower, pen your dog in, put it in a crate, leave it in a tiled room or take it with you.
· Start to observe what your dog's signs and signals are before they toilet. Some sniff, some circle, some start to get

Time	Food	Drink	Wee	Poo	Accident
7 a.m.					
8 a.m.					
9 a.m.					
10 a.m.					
11 a.m.					
Midday					
1 p.m.					
2 p.m.					
3 p.m.					
4 p.m.					
5 p.m.					
6 p.m.					
7 p.m.					
8 p.m.					
9 p.m.					
10 p.m.					
11 p.m.					
Midnight					

frantic, some squeak, it really does vary and, as soon as you see it, take it outside. My dog used to do what we called 'the poo dance' as when she needed to go, she would start running around, skipping, jumping and throwing herself against walls until she found the right spot. That made it very easy to work out!

· If your dog starts to pee or poo, walk away, do not give your dog any attention – ignore it. (Do not tell it off, shout it at it and certainly don't pick it up and start to move your dog outside. If you constantly tell your dog off, you are much more likely to end up with a dog that hides to toilet or starts to eat its own poo, as you have made it so scared of going to the toilet in front of you.)

· Try to clear up any accidents when the dog is out of the room, the least attention drawn to it the better.

· Make sure you mop the area with either a shop-bought dog detergent or just mix up half a quantity of biological washing powder and half of hot water. Be fastidious in the cleaning up process – you don't want them repeat-marking in the middle of your lovely parquet flooring just because they can smell themselves from the previous accident!

· Take any soft furnishings up off the floor. Your dog cannot determine between the cheap Ikea rug and the £3,000 Persian one.

When you are in the home, you need to be either picking your dog up or walking your dog into the garden/street/park every half an hour to toilet. Every hour maximum. Otherwise you will continue to get accidents. Toilet training is all about the opportunities given.

· Fill in the timetable opposite for a week. You will start to build up a picture of your dog's toilet schedule.

· Keep set meal times and if your dog doesn't finish its meal, pick it up until the next meal time. If they are grazing, you won't be able to predict when they will need to poo, as you won't know how much and when they ate.

· Always take your dog outside to toilet as soon as they wake up, if they have been doing energetic play, have just eaten or drank.

OUT IN THE BIG WIDE WORLD

· Allow your dog somewhere to sniff and explore – it's a dog not a robot.

· If your dog poos in the area you want it to, on your private property, leave it there so that the area smells of your dog when you next visit. Of course, if the poo in a public space it needs to be picked up.

· If your dog goes to the toilet outside, act like someone has just presented you with a big, hefty cheque. I want to see treats, stroking, kind words, dancing up and down. The whole lot to tell your dog that what it did was right. You are creating the exact opposite of what happens if it toilets in the house.

· Always carry more poo bags then you can ever think you might need!

· In the city, as owners we usually have to walk down a street to get to a park. And it's always on these busy streets, pedestrian crossings or by someone's front door that our dogs will decide it's the perfect time to go for a huge poo. If you have access to a garden, try and get your dog to poo in there before you leave. It's much easier and far less hassle.

· If your dog is a rescue dog it might have a real preference for a particular surface, which can be difficult living in an urban environment. Very slowly try to introduce them to other surfaces. If they favour grass, walk them on a grass verge so that you can gradually move them off. For a dog to be reliant only on one surface for toileting can be especially difficult in a city.

MOUTHING AND NIPPING

For me, a dog's mouth, teeth and human skin shouldn't meet. Your dog should not need to bite. However, with puppies it's a bit different – you may be reading this with lovely little puppy chasing you around your living room trying to eat your slippers, feet, laces and trousers. Puppies grow teeth and it hurts them. A great deal. With children we can dish out a mild pain killer and put the amber teething beads on them, but you can't give human pain killers to dogs! Instead, their bodies release a natural pain killer every time their teeth make contact with something – so eating your slippers, feet and the like helps relieve the pain. But this certainly doesn't help you when their little needles of pain are hanging off of your hand when you're just trying to tie up your shoelaces.

You need to get very efficient with your puppy's biting incidents. Pin a piece of paper to the fridge where everyone has access to it and make a note of any times in the day when your dog gets nippy. Write down what was happening, who was involved, what your dog did and what you tried to do (see opposite). This is to determine a schedule of biting and will enable you to work out when your dog seems to be at its worst, and what worked, what didn't or what made it even worse. It also allows you to sit back and evaluate the patterns over a G&T when you are a bit calmer. Usually these biting attacks will take place first thing in the morning when everyone comes into the room, around 7 p.m. at night and often at other points during the day.

Sometimes it can be because your dog has too much energy, has just woken up, is bored or hasn't had enough exercise. But you need to fathom this out. I once visited a Patterdale terrier puppy who was fourteen weeks old and the vet had scared the owners into not even letting the dog into their secure garden. They were having huge problems with biting. As soon as we got her outside, exercising and stimulated, she totally calmed down. Her biting was her way of saying that something wasn't right.

If you find the biting is purely down to teething then you can introduce some teething toys or activities, just as we do with babies. Broccoli stalks, cold carrots from the freezer and ice cubes are brilliant (more ideas overleaf). As are shop bought items like rawhide and raw marrow bones from the butcher. It's then all about choosing the right times to give these to your dog. For example, if you get up in the morning and your dog is like a fully charged iPhone battery, ready to conquer the world, now would be a good time to put it out in the garden/crate/bed with a raw marrow bone that it can happily take all that teething energy out on.

Date	Place	Who was involved	What was happening	What your dog did	What you tried to do

You are trying to redirect the teething behaviour before your dog finds his own way of doing it.

I often hear that a puppy should be allowed to play bite as it is only young. If you have taken your puppy from a reputable and decent breeder, your puppy should already have learnt that biting isn't tolerated. No nursing mother will allow her litter to chew on her, bite her or teeth on her nipples; she will let her puppies know they have done something wrong. It is your role to continue this education. Allowing your puppy to teeth on you and other dogs ruins all that hard work your puppy's mother put in. In my opinion, a dog's teeth should never make contact with human skin.

FUN CHEWING IDEAS

Here are some ideas that can provide your puppy with the relief it needs, to relieve the pain, stimulate them and tire them out. Meaning that you can get on with some work, or just go to the toilet or sit down and have a cup of tea.

With all of these ideas, make sure you put your dog in its crate on a wipeable surface, as all of them are fairly messy. They are well woth it though!

ICE BALLS

Take some raw meat or wet dog food, and with a spoon make it into little balls. You can even stuff the middle with an extra little treat if you like. Now place each ball into an egg box and pop into the freezer until frozen solid. Take one out and give it to your puppy to bat around, teeth on and chew up. If you have a large breed use a bigger mould, otherwise they could just swallow these whole.

BOX FRESH

Take a cardboard box and, using a corkscrew, make some holes in the sides. On one side fill the holes with small, smelly treats. On another, thread a piece of tough fabric through the holes, as if you are sewing. Tie the ends but leave some fabric hanging. On the third side make a bigger hole and wedge a toy through it. And then let your puppy get on with it. Your puppy should adore pulling, chewing, teething and generally battering the hell out of it.

BANANA-RAMA

Peel a banana, coat in honey and freeze it. Especially brilliant for a hot day. To make it into more of an ice lolly-type treat, stick a rawhide chew in the end when freezing.

STOCK UP

Make some ice cubes up made from weak chicken, vegetable or beef stock and freeze.

VEG GALORE

This is a great one if your dog loves fruit and vegetables. Wash items like a carrot, broccoli stalk and segments of apples, and don't dry them off. Place in the freezer so that the water you washed them in freezes on the outside of the veg. Then give to your dog to chew on. Many will eat it up which is also fine. Or they may just destroy it by chewing it and shredding it into a zillion and one pieces. Have a dustpan and brush handy.

8.

TRAINING ESSENTIALS

Owning and living with a dog in the city requires any dog to have manners and to know some commands to some extent. A well-mannered dog is adored by all and I do not mean a robot dog. I like a dog to have a personality and a sense of its own free will, but I also want it to be safe, liked and a great addition to the city and local community. I believe there are a few commands which make life far more enjoyable if you can teach your dog and these, for me, are the following:

- Greet people correctly – not jump up
- Come when called, also known as recall
- Walk well on a lead
- Wait
- Leave
- Sit
- Down
- To react well to cars, children and other dogs

This book has not been written as a training manual as there wouldn't be space to fit everything in. But if you are seeking out a trainer and behaviourist to work with, I advise the following:

- Look for someone who is a trainer *and* behaviourist, as I don't see how you can teach a dog if you don't understand their behaviour.

- Find someone that you really like and get on with, it has to be the right fit for you.
- Never, ever accept anyone utilising techniques that scare, shock or make your dog fearful, such as choke chains, prong collars, electric collars or domination systems such as alpha rolls.
- Seek out someone who lives a life similar to yours. If I got asked to teach Border collies to herd sheep on a farm I wouldn't know where to start. It isn't the life I lead or an area where I have any experience.
- There are various bodies in different countries who have members, you can consult these if you agree with their ethos. In the UK the Kennel Club have set up a standardised membership system, this may not be the same everywhere else.
- Ask to observe a class or lesson to check you like the trainer's style.

The crucial thing to remember is that dog training is not quick and it isn't instant. I rely on clients doing their homework and putting in the time and effort it requires. You are paying for someone's knowledge as well as their service – while your budget is obviously a factor, you are better to find the right person for you and your dog, not just the cheapest person. A well-trained dog is all the more enjoyable a companion. Knowing that you can take them to most places makes life much easier.

MOTIVATORS

The best way to teach your dog anything is to have motivators, and working them out for each dog is one of the biggest parts of my job.

Every single human, whether adult or child, has things that get them motivated. This is also is true for dogs. If you are training your dog and wonder why she isn't 'getting it', it's usually because you haven't found the right motivator.

Think of it in the same way as if I was asking you to do a really hard task but I wasn't willing to pay you, take you out for dinner or buy you any chocolate. After a while you would get bored and lose interest.

For us to make sure that a dog wants to learn what we have to teach them, we have to find out the right thing to use. Some dogs love treats, others love toys, some just want a cuddle, others a combination of them all. On top of this, each and every dog has their own quirky little things that get them excited, that rev them up and make them want to get involved.

To get you thinking, here are a few of Cookie's motivators. As she's deaf, I cannot use my voice or noisy toys, but there are still many things that get her going and my body language is key. In no particular order:

- Cheese
- Tennis ball
- Me
- Rough and tumble play
- Running through my legs
- Climbing on tree trunks
- Liver cake
- Rubber toy stuffed with treats
- Having her chin rubbed up and down

Once you know what your dog likes, you have to work out how to use it. I once fostered a beautiful boxer cross Great Dane called Henry. He was found during the London riots and when he came to me he was like a tearaway child! One of the things that I discovered he adored was to play in the big piles of leaves that build up in parks. His recall was very difficult to work on but the leaves formed part of his reward. He would come running back and, in return, I would throw the leaves in the air for him to play with. Yet my own dog, Cookie, would stand watching, with no interest whatsoever. Sometimes you need to forget your preconceptions of what a dog *should* like and spend time working out what they *do* love, like, don't mind and can't bear. When you know these things you hold the key to good behaviour in the palm of your hand!

TREATS

There are a huge range of these out on the market, you can buy them in corner shops, supermarkets, boutiques and online. It's worth spending some time to find decent chews and more durable items, but for bite-size training treats the more natural the better. I've never met a dog that didn't adore frankfurters, sausages, ham, chicken and cheese. For more portable snacks, check out the kids' snack section in the refrigerated aisles, they usually do items in individually wrapped small versions of all of these – perfect for the park.

TOYS

What constitutes a toy depends on your imagination. You can, of course, utilise the array of genius items that are on the market, but don't be caught up in only using these. Depending on your breed or the nature of your dog, many a household item can make a wonderful toy. I love it when I see owners making use of things others wouldn't think of. If your dog adores the plastic ladle that you don't use any more, who are we to say that isn't a great toy to fetch and retrieve? The world is your oyster when it comes to toys. Be creative. As long as your dog enjoys playing with it it's fair game.

GAMES

This is where understanding and knowing your dog is crucial, as what one dog hates another will love. Don't assume that your dog, if it is a particular breed, will only play in one way. It is up to you to channel their 'way' of playing into the right way. Like I've said, Cookie adores running through my legs like a tunnel when she recalls back to me. As she goes through, I squidge her tail and she turns around and runs right back through again. For her this is brilliant, for another dog it wouldn't be. Take the time to play and discover what is at the heart of your dog.

A HIERARCHY OF MOTIVATION

Now you have your list of what your dog loves, you need to make them work for it. Work out what they find amazing and what is just nice. If every time your dog sits, you dish out a chunk of the finest cheddar, but then you use the same treat when you are trying to teach them something much trickier, the two rewards for the tasks don't equate. It is like me asking you to work for an hour and then for an entire day for the same amount of money. It doesn't make sense.

You hold the key to your dog's motivations, so it is now up to you to use these incredibly powerful things in the right way. Make life fun for your dog and they will want to learn, make life boring and they will shy away from training with you.

USING PAIN OR FEAR AS MOTIVATOR

There are still some schools of thought out there that will advocate the use of pain as a system of training. Times have changed and it's been proven that in order to teach a dog to do something, using motivators is the best way forward.

A dog that is scared, worried, anxious or fearful will find it very hard to concentrate on a task. How would you feel if, when you got something wrong, your teacher hit you around the head with a chain? In my experience, if you can turn a training exercise into a game, you will enjoy it more and so will your beloved dog.

When you have fun with your dog, your relationship strengthens, you gain more trust in each other and you are able to move a step closer to your goal. When you put an electric collar on your dog to stop it barking, you lose the ability to look at what created the problem.

It's not to say that some equipment doesn't have a place in life-threatening situations, but every dog's behaviour has a reason behind it. Take the time to pull the puzzle to pieces and you can put it back together again in the right way. It does take a great deal of time and patience, and in today's busy urban society, many people are time short – but that's not a reason to take shortcuts, owning a dog is a time-consuming hobby. As with so many things in life, put in a lot and you'll get a lot back. Having a dog can be truly rewarding, but you need to put time, love and patience into it.

9.

GIVE ME
A SIGN

As dog owners we need to understand what our dogs are trying to tell us. Never more than in the city, our dogs will ask us to get them out of sticky situations or to remove them from something that they really dislike.

Unfortunately for dogs and for us, we communicate in totally different ways. If your partner yawns, you think they're tired or bored, but if your dog yawns that's incorrect.

Your dog will face hundreds of situations every week and if we can understand what they're communicating, we can help them. Imagine a group of school kids surrounding your dog, a dog running up to your dog, a busy bus journey with many hands trying to touch your dog. If you can respond to how your dog is feeling, you should dramatically reduce the need for them to bite, nip and growl.

Puppies, an adult dog or an elderly dog all communicate to each other in the same way. They learnt it as a tiny puppy (providing they were raised correctly) when with their litter and mother. The problems arise for dog communication when we humans totally misread their signals. We can end up punishing or ignoring our dogs just for trying to tell us something – and this means the dog has to find quicker and more efficient ways to let you know how they feel.

I find the easiest way to think of the ways dogs communicate is to look at the ways we do so and compare them. I'll use the traffic light system – Green, Amber and Red – to differentiate the urgency of each communication.

HUMAN COMMUNICATION

Imagine you are stood on a busy bus. Another passenger keeps standing too close, touching you, infringing on your space and being very rude.

GREEN

- You sigh and frown.
- You step away from the passenger.
- You put your bag between you and them.
- You try to move to a different area of the bus.

AMBER

- You ask the passenger to move away but the he ignores your signals so you move to amber.
- You stick an elbow out to make it more uncomfortable to stand close.

- You tell them that they are making you uncomfortable.
- Now annoyed, your face starts to go red and your breathing becomes heavier.
- You start to feel hot and stressed.

RED

- Passenger ignores amber signals so your adrenaline starts to pump and you get angry, moving to the red zone.
- Some humans may shout and swear.
- They may push them away with force.
- They may attempt to hit them or use physical strength.

DOG COMMUNICATION

Now imagine a child very interested in sitting next to your dog and petting its face and body. Your dog also utllises signals to let the child know how it feels.

GREEN

- Dog turns its face away.
- Doesn't make eye contact.
- Licks its lips repeatedly.
- Sniffs the ground.
- Dog creates distance between him and the child.

AMBER

- Dog starts to pant and yawns.
- Dog does a body shake to relieve stress.
- Some dogs do a lip curl to show teeth.
- Walks away.
- Breathing may change.
- Child now follows the dog when it walks away and continues to pester.

RED

- If child still follows and insists on invading the dog's space the dog may growl.
- Dog may lunge.
- Some dogs will nip or bite.
- There are then five types of bites which can be administered from minor to major.

Whatever the situation, and whether you are human or canine, we will all find a way to let others know how we are feeling. With a dog, if we keep ignoring the Green and Amber signs, the dog begins to realise that this gentle, calm system of communicating is inefficient. It doesn't get them what they want which, in this case, is for the child to leave them alone.

If these situations keep arising and the child continues with this pestering but the dog's behaviour remains unacknowledged, it will creep up the traffic light system. And when it reaches the Red, we humans consider this to be 'aggressive behaviour' which is bad and unacceptable. The problem is that once the dog realises the Red behaviour is more efficient they are more likely to revert to it to achieve their end goal, to get the child to back off.

As I see it, if more owners took the time to understand what their dog is trying to tell them, we would have far more dogs staying in homes and not being rehomed, abandoned and put down.

Some of the Green and Amber signs are quite subtle, so here are some drawings that can help you start to see exactly what your dog is doing and why. Remember, each dog is different and breed specifics can play a role. The more time you invest in your dog the quicker you will 'get it', and soon you will be hanging around your local park pointing out what everyone else's dog is thinking and doing – something I find hard not to do, even when sat in the pub having a drink!

All of these postures and signs are applicable to when dogs communicate with a human or a dog. The key to it all is taking action. When your dog tells you it is scared, move it away. When your dog is fearful, give it space, when your dog is anxious allow it to calm down and when it is happy and wiggling away, wiggle back and have some fun!

I'm not sure

I'm worried and need space

Let's play!

I feel anxious

I'm reactive

I'm trying to make myself disappear

I'm on alert

I'm happy to see you

Please back off

TAIL POSITIONS

Helicopter tail Where it circles like a propeller, you can't stop it and it has the most energy behind it. It is usually reserved for the dog's most favourite people in the world.

Wiggling tail This is what you receive when you get home from work, a wiggling tail that indicates how pleased your dog is to see you.

Rigid, upright tail Usually used during information gathering when a dog isn't sure. If the entire body is stiff, it can indicate that an aggressive display may follow.

Ticking tail Picture a slow, ticking arm of a clock, the tail does the same thing. There is tension and it will go one of two ways – both dogs could move away and walk off or a squabble could start.

Tucked A dog's version of hiding, it removes the ability of another dog to sniff their scent and so makes them feel like they have removed themselves from the situation.

THE EYES

You learn a lot from a dog's eyes. They aren't just simply opened or closed.

Larger than normal Can indicate that a dog is scared or anxious, which may result in aggression or trying to get as far away from what is worrying them.

Smaller than normal Dogs who are ill or in pain will often squint or make their eyes smaller than usual.

Whale eye The dog will look at a potential threat – human or a dog – and a large area of the white of the eye will be seen. May result in an aggressive display. You frequently see it when a dog is guarding something or is being forced into a situation they really don't feel comfortable being in.

THE EARS

The breed of your dog obviously plays a role in this as different dogs have very different sizes and ear positions. However, usually their reactions are the same, some you just have to work harder to notice.

Relaxed position Exactly as it says.

Flattened to the head Looks as if someone has combed them back, usually indicates a dog that is anxious, worried or frightened.

Upright A dog that is on alert. Look out for potential aggressive displays or running away, but all could be fine – the dog might relax as, for example, the person approaching is a known friend or the perceived threat disappears.

Raised and forward Potential aggression to follow.

THE MOUTH

The smile Many say that a dog can't smile but I would disagree, I've met lots of dogs who have used their mouth to show just how happy they are to see you. Their smile is soft, relaxed and accompanied by the helicopter tail and relaxed posture.

Tense mouth Often accompanied by a low growling, a very clear warning signal that there is something the dog is not happy about.

Panting If in hot weather it is self-explanatory, otherwise it is a sign that a dog is feeling stressed. We often see this with dogs in rehoming blocks.

Lip curl Is when the dog shows teeth, it is similar to when Elvis used to do his 'uh huh' lip curl, except it's done as a warning! A lip curl is a very clear indicator, the dog is telling you to back off.

Puffing I mostly see this with dogs who are put in situations they find hard to cope with. Their mouth puffs out at the sides and it's accompanied by deeper breathing.

THE WHOLE PICTURE

When looking at your dog, it's not about taking into account just one of the above signals. You have to put the whole picture together and look at the situation your dog is reacting to. You may also find that some dogs will start to use a particular display and if you don't pay attention they will add others in to make you sit up and take notice.

10.

URBAN ETIQUETTE

Working in a busy city with dogs has made me realise just how tiring it can be for them. We humans understand what all the stimulus are, but they do not. There are a few rules that will help you and your dog live a far more enjoyable life in town.

· You do not have to take your dog everywhere, most dogs would prefer to be asleep in their 'bed of joy' than lying under your table in a bar while you and your friends do a three-hour pub quiz. Wooden, alcohol-soaked floors aren't the comfiest place to lounge.

· If you are travelling on public transport, pick an inside seat and try to position your dog underneath the chair or between your legs for their safety.

· Do not allow your dog to meet and greet every dog, on or off lead. I don't do that to every person I see so I don't expect my dog to.

· Always carry your dog on escalators, the thought of their paw nails getting caught is unbearable.

· If you do take your dog to a cafe or bar, do not allow your dog to sprawl over the pavement. Tuck your dog under your table, in a corner or against a wall. For their safety and sense of security as much as anything.

· Remember that we have to share our spaces with other people so be respectful that not everyone loves dogs like we do, and don't give them a good reason for disliking dogs by allowing yours to be badly behaved.

YOUR DOG, THE AMBASSADOR

The biggest issue we face in cities with dogs is that *some* dog owners are giving non-dog owners too many reasons to restrict us all. In the city we have to share space, and this means being considerate that the areas need to be used by all. Far too often I witness owners allowing their dogs to play so roughly that a child would be scared. Or I see owners allowing their dogs to jump all over people or terrorise picnics and steal food, which is simply unacceptable. No dog or human is perfect but let's at least show people we are trying to be great dog owners.

Each owner and their dog needs to be an ambassador. We need to show people what a wonderful addition dogs can be to society. The law changes from country to country and state to state, but in the UK you can be penalised for your dog being out of control, which can result in your dog being seized and restrictions placed on it for the rest of its waking days.

A dog walk should be just that, a walk to benefit your dog. But if you are going to take your dog into public domains – a public park, a busy street, on transport or in cafes – you need to train your dog how to behave in a way that is acceptable.

Teaching a dog how to behave in a human environment takes a huge amount of time, energy and patience. Bear in mind that you cannot have a perfect dog, in the same way that you cannot be a perfect human, but we can be constantly working to show how fantastic dogs can be in the city.

Occasionally something will go wrong or not according to plan, and all we can ask is that we learn from these incidents.

SOCIALISATION IN THE CITY

Whether you own a puppy or a rescue dog, you need to try and find out what they have already seen, met, done and experienced. Obviously you cannot find out every single thing, but to know if there is something that worries your new rescue dog will help you enormously.

If you have just brought your puppy home, at the right time, you should be now thinking about how to socialise it. For me, the socialisation process is often done incorrectly. The six-to-twelve-weeks-old period is there to allow you to

teach your dog about the things that will feature in its new life. So if you live in an urban environment, you have a great deal to get done.

With a rescue dog, the socialisation timescale is often determined by the individual dog, as it will come down to its age, its previous experiences and environment. There are no hard and fast rules like the key socialisation period for a puppy.

With a puppy or a rescue, you need to be very careful not to 'flood' your dog by doing too much and scaring them. Every new experience should come in short bursts and built up slowly. This is also a learning curve for you, to find out about your new friend's concerns, likes, loves and uncertainties. It is also key to making these experiences as positive as possible.

This is not an exhaustive list but it is to give you an idea on some of the areas, people and things you might need to expose your puppy to. Remember, you need to tailor this list to your lifestyle.

TRAVELLING

- Bus
- Underground/subway
- Train
- Boat
- Car
- By bike (whether your dog is small enough to go in the basket or fast enough to run alongside)

PEOPLE

- Men
- Women
- Babies
- Toddlers
- Children
- Men with beards
- Elderly people with walking sticks
- People wearing glasses/hats
- Children on scooters
- Dog owners walking their dogs on lead/off lead
- Workers in uniforms e.g. police

EQUIPMENT

- Bikes
- Pushchairs/buggies
- Wheelchairs
- Scooters
- Motorbikes

PLACES

- Your favourite pub
- Your workplace
- Local market
- The park
- The vet
- A cafe
- Dog groomers
- Local shops that allow dogs
- School gates

When your dog exhibits behaviour to say it has had enough, is worried or doesn't want to do something, you must take note. Some of the biggest problems I find when working with adult dogs stem from puppyhood.

Whether you have a rescue dog that you know is scared of men or you have a puppy that you are just trying to introduce everyone to, caution is everything. If, on the other hand, you spend time trying to give your dog positive associations around something, it can really pay off. I am not a believer in pairing food with fear. If you have a dog scared or reacting aggressively to a situation, please follow your behaviourist's instructions carefully, using food with a great deal of caution. If food is used incorrectly, you can end up either rewarding the behaviour you don't want or you can make the dog more intent on getting the food and then reacting.

SOCIALISATION WITH ADULTS

One of the keys to making your dog think that in general people are good is to show them. Dogs are clever and they form associations with certain people for certain things. If there are key people in your life that you would like your dog to be friends with, ensure that those associations are positive. For instance, it may be that they get involved in feeding your dog, walking your dog, playing with your dog in the park, throwing the ball in the home. Dogs are quite simple and they constantly strive to make us humans meet their needs.

But you also reap what you sow. For example, when a client's dog as a puppy kept being forced by a housemate to do rough and tumble play that she hated, she eventually formed the opinion that

this person wasn't fun to be around – that fundamentally he scared her. Now every time he comes over, she retreats to her crate and won't come out. She is clever because she now avoids a situation with someone who she associates with discomfort and fear.

As well as your close friends and family, you will want your dog to socialise with other adults. If you need to talk to a person, the best thing you can do is to show your dog what you would like them to do, which in an ideal world is to sit next to you and wait. In a city, you don't want your dog to jump up at people when they meet them, so don't allow it. Don't allow them to do it with strangers in the park.

Some people will ask to meet her. Others won't ask and they just start touching, and you need to stop them. Your dog is your responsibility and if you allow people to manhandle or touch them in a way you are not happy about it, it will only escalate. A dog will only learn to be scared or wary of humans if certain behaviours happen over and over again when they are near. So if every time your dog meets people, they crowd him, get in his face and pat the top of his head it would be understandable if he developed a dislike people on the street. Too often new owners get caught up in feeling proud that people want to say hi to their dog, and the actual dog gets forgotten.

I find the best way of taking control of the situation is to ask those who want to meet your dog to do something – you could give the person a treat, and ask them to ask your dog to sit, or you could drop treats on the floor while they pet the dog. However, if your dog is a resource guarder, a fearful dog or food aggressive, you must avoid these situations.

Always check if your dog wants to socialise. If your dog is sat behind your legs or under the chair, it is quite clearly telling you that it is not happy to interact and wants to be left alone. Forcing your dog out or to interact will either immediately or eventually lead to issues.

SOCIALISATION WITH CHILDREN

This is one of the hardest things to get right as children are unpredictable, erratic and often smell delicious! You have to make the child's safety your priority. You cannot take risks involving children, they are relying on you to make the right decisions for them.

Much of the socialisation is similar as it is with adults; it is about giving the dog some space and creating positive situations. There are some key rules that should be put into place around our four-legged friends and our two-legged mini-humans.

· Children should not be allowed to hit, jump on, sit on or provoke a dog. Both a dog and a child have boundaries and they both require consideration and respect.
· When a dog is in its bed, a child should never be allowed to invade their space.
· When a dog is sleeping, never, ever allow a child to wake a dog. A dog startled or scared can react in a way that isn't pleasant. If you imagine being fast asleep in your bed and I jump on your chest, your first instinct would not be to say hi

and give me a cuddle. It would involve screaming, swearing and possibly some physical repercussions. The dog equivalent to this is biting your child, potentially in the face.

· A child should never be allowed to touch, mess with or be too close to a dog eating. No matter how well-mannered your dog.

· If you feed bones and chews, please do it when your dog is able to be left alone or can be put outside or separate from children. These items can be high value and sometimes worth guarding. And I can guarantee that if putting a child up against a dog with a bone, the child will end up worse off.

· As lovely as it seems to let your toddler hold the lead of your dog as you walk down the street, in a city it isn't wise. One pull towards a discarded chicken bone and your child is on the floor while the dog is gobbling down his prize. Practise in the house or garden if you have one with no distractions, it is much safer.

· Lastly, never under any circumstances leave a dog alone with a child. You cannot trust a dog, it is an animal and you cannot trust a child to make the right decisions. It isn't worth the risk but secondly the potential of what could happen if your dog got scared or anxious doesn't bear thinking about.

I once met a dog that was hiding under the kitchen table every time the child came into the room. It turned out there had been an incident where the mum had left the two alone and found the three-year-old trying to put Lego down the dog's ear canals. This dog was being incredibly restrained by removing herself each time the child was around, and there was a reason. Please remember to respect your dog's boundaries.

SOCIALISATION WITH OTHER DOGS

When you live in a busy environment, any time that you visit a green space or dog-friendly walking area you are virtually guaranteed to come into contact with other dogs. It is essential that your dog can be around other members of the canine species, but they don't need to be 'friends' with every dog they come into contact with – this is where many problems can develop. To your dog to socialise well, implement the following:

· A dog walk in the park should be about you and your dog. Base it around rewards, playtime and interaction with you.

· Don't stop to say 'Hi' and pet every dog you meet in the park. Teach your dog to walk on past and ignore them, rewarding them when they do.

· Seek out older dogs who you view as great role models and walk with them occasionally. By role models I mean the ones who are not bothered about your dog and just want to do their own thing and focus on their owner. Your dog can learn a great deal from them.

· If you are going to walk for an hour, then interactions and play times with other dogs should make up less than 10 per cent of the walk.

· Avoid walking regularly in large groups, as it really doesn't permit any interaction between you and your dog.

· If you have a very athletic, high-energy dog, instead of just allowing it to burn energy off with other dogs it would be far better to redirect this into training your dog to run with you or run alongside as you cycle. Or teach them a game to utilise in the park such as 'find it' or 'hide and seek'.

· If in doubt, make use of a ten-metre training line so your dog enjoys some freedom but you remain in control.

· Avoid your dog on lead meeting and greeting other dogs. You are far more likely to end up with lead aggression if you persist with this.

· Make sure you vary the walks you do.

Just because a park is nearest, doesn't mean it's always the right park for you.

What owners lose sight of is that, generally, if your dog was born to a good mother and part of a litter with siblings, your dog learnt how to be a dog the day it was born. The issues usually arise when as owners we interfere and start to complicate the process.

For example, I recently met a gorgeous Border terrier who was just over a year old. From twelve weeks old he had been walked in a big group with other dogs, who he played with continuously while the owners chatted en route around the park. Coffee in hand, obviously – no dog owner in London ventures into the park on a cold day without a takeaway coffee! When they came to me, the owners were getting frustrated that their dog wouldn't come back to them when they called him, that dogs were the things he was most distracted by. Yet he was only carrying out what they had taught him – to go to the park and seek out, like a heat-seeking missile, the other dogs to play with.

In my opinion, a dog walk should be just that. A walk that you do with your dog. Ideally, your dog should be polite to other dogs, but you should be his main focus.

You only need two to three incidents of dog-on-dog aggression before a dog starts to generalise some of this and become reactive. Treatment is harder than prevention, so please put the time in to create a happy and balanced dog from the outset. When you take on a puppy or a rescue dog, the rules and boundaries you put in place *now* affect the future. So if you would like a dog that comes back to you in the park, doesn't fight with other dogs and isn't running off to hunt out any other four-legged hounds, then you need to teach them what you do expect from the very beginning.

TRAVELLING IN THE CITY

You will need to teach your dog how you would like them to behave when travelling, but bear in mind that your dog isn't a human who can predict what situations may arise, so you will always need to be your dog's eyes and ears. Keep an eye on people around you, what they are doing, the bags they are carrying and what their opinion is of dogs being on public transport. When I was travelling on the bus with Cookie and Henry, an elderly lady who didn't believe they should be on the bus repeatedly tried to ram their paws with her shopping trolley. The dogs were lying on the floor, in nobody's way. It was certainly a lesson that not everyone is keen on your dog travelling beside them. I did confront the woman and placed my legs in front of my dogs. I expect my dogs to be treated with respect, even by those who don't wish to own one themselves.

A great item to travel with is a blanket that is light, easy to carry and easy to wash. Start to train your dog to always sit on it when it is available. If it offers some cushioning then your dog should choose to use it in preference to a cold, hard floor and its familiarity will offer some comfort in new places. Unless of course it is the summer – when a cold floor is definitely preferable.

BUS

This is one of the easiest ways to travel with your dog, as if it gets too busy, if you need some air or a dog gets on that doesn't react well to your dog, then you can very easily just hop off the bus. I always try to get a seat where I can tuck the dog under the seat next to the wall, so they cannot get trampled on, run over or scared. Always let people know when they sit down that you do have a dog under the seat as some people really object when your dog moves to get more comfortable. I avoid going upstairs as coming back down the steps when the bus is grinding

to a halt can be a bit fraught. You also always never know what you are walking your dog into as you come down the steps to the ground floor of the bus. In the UK, a bus driver does have the right to insist where you sit. They usually won't but, if it is really busy they may try to.

UNDERGROUND OR SUBWAY

This is one of the craziest places to bring your dog because it isn't just about the getting on the train. Before they even embark they must enter the station, go through a turnstile, go down an escalator, in a lift or stairs, stand and wait on a busy platform until a train arrives. Then they can finally get on. It is a great amount to deal with and understand. And then you have the scents that accompany such an experience.

If you own a puppy, start gradually by introducing them to many of these aspects individually. If they are a pup in arms, then you can do much of it very easily. If you have a rescue or a bigger dog then you need to make sure that they are comfortable first with individual parts of it. For example, you need to know that your huge Rottweiler cross is happy to be scooped up and carried while you stand on the longest escalator ever with people staring and trying to pet him as they go past. Travelling with my bulldog can be back-breaking work, especially if I'm with my baby too! You really have to think about your journeys – arriving at a station with no lift when you have a buggy, baby and dog is terrible news.

When you're ready to get on the train, if it is absolutely packed I advise waiting for the next train. You want to find a space to stand or sit that you are happy with – one heavy-footed passenger can easily break a bone in a delicate-framed dog like a whippet, or trample a small dog like a pug. If your dog is small enough, your lap is the ideal sleeping spot, you can wrap them in a scarf out of touching's way and let them chill out. If your dog is medium-sized like mine, I make her sit under my legs so that my feet are protecting her from getting stood on. If you have a large breed dog, I'd find a corner in a carriage and, again, put them either behind you or between your legs with your hand down the back of their collar and holding onto their lead for their reassurance.

BOAT

In some cities using the river is a great way to travel. Bear in mind that most boats are made of metal, which means that decks, ramps and seating areas can get damp, slippery and cold. It can disorientate them if these kinds of surfaces are unfamiliar.

Many of the boats I've travelled on have bench-type seats, so I try to sit at the back, at the end of a bench nearest the wall of the boat, and tuck my dog under the seat. If your dog loves to look out, then by all means let them sit on your knee and look out, as long as they don't bark at everything passing and that they are not snappy with people – a dog sat on a lap looks appealing for the public to approach.

TAXI

In London, most black cabs are really dog-friendly, they love to have a chat about your dog and tell you about theirs. When you use minicabs you really do need to check on booking if they will accept a dog. Not all drivers will.

In the cab, your dog sits between your legs in the foot well, so that if they are muddy, dirty or shedding fur it is easy to clear it up. If you have a small breed then it curling up on your lap is acceptable too. I don't think it is acceptable to let your dog up onto the seats so it can look out of the window. It may love doing this in your car, but this *isn't* your car. It's important we encourage taxi drivers to think that dogs are acceptable passengers – I normally give a bit extra as a tip too.

If for any reason your dog suffers from car sickness, avoid using a taxi if you can. If you're desperate and need to get them to the vet, then cover the floor in blankets – so that if there is an accident, you can wrap the blankets up and remove everything when you exit.

No matter how well behaved or experienced a dog, they can still get scared by something unexpected, and you need to make sure you are prepared if this does happen. If for any reason you are unsure of your dog's reaction, or you are travelling when they have had medication (e.g. after an anaesthetic), then I would suggest putting a basket muzzle on for everyone's safety. Your dog can still eat and drink out of them. It also means that if your dog is touch sensitive, it should make people think twice and leave your dog alone.

WHAT MAKES A DANGEROUS DOG

When you live in a densely populated environment, it's unfortunately highly likely that you will encounter a dog that you could consider dangerous – i.e., that it may intimidate, scare, attack or injure you or your dog. Know what to look for and then avoid the dogs.

The best thing to look out for is the

owner, not the dog. In my experience, a dangerous dog is created when an owner neglects to give a dog what it requires. All dogs require love, care, food, water, socialisation, exercise and stimulation. When you start to remove these or add in things like pain, beating, hitting, shouting and scolding, you begin to change the ability of a dog to be balanced. An out-of-balance dog that is scared, anxious, worried or confused will react to 'things' in the outside world. Generally speaking it is usually down to human error that a dog has ended up being dangerous – whether it is through poor breeding and raising, through being beaten, being starved or from not being exercised.

A breed doesn't symbolise a dangerous dog, a type of person does. And that isn't down to what they wear, how much they earn, what race they are or anything similar. It is down to how they treat their dog.

To give you an idea, here are some of the people I would avoid when walking my city streets:

· The owner on the phone with its dog off lead – owner can't be paying any attention to what their dog is doing or where it is. It may not be dangerous, but the owner will not be capable of controlling it, so if it is dangerous you are in trouble.
· The one carrying a great metal chain lead around its fist doesn't bode well.

· The person screaming and swearing at their kids as they walk the dog around the park. If they shout at and push their children around, what will they do to their dog?
· The group of owners walking their dogs while they chat with a coffee. They are not focused on their dogs, who could be off and out of control, racing up to your dog as you walk it on lead.
· The person beating their dog in public for not coming when called. Don't just stand and tut, call the police and stand up for a dog.
· Lastly, if you see a person who doesn't pick up their dog's poo, in my opinion it's debatable how much they care about dogs. Dog poo can make children go blind and can be dangerous to other dogs – if you have such little care for others in the world, will you really be caring that much about your own dog?

If you are in any doubt about a dog, call your dog away, walk past and give it a wide birth. Do not under any circumstances 'wait to see what happens' – if it goes wrong, potentially you and your dog could be the ones coming off worse for wear. I speak from experience – a man approached my friend and I when we were ordering coffees. He tried to get involved in our conversation and started to try and show us his underwear. We asked him to leave and went to sit around the corner at a table. The man appeared to walk off but then turned and came back towards us, attacking my friend, punching me and choking my dog until she was unconscious.

A great tip I was taught by a policeman and dog handler is to carry a small bottle of hairspray with you. If a dog goes to attack, or it looks likely, spraying it in the face area of an offending dog may help. It's not guaranteed, but it could be enough to break the moment and give you time to make a swift exit. There are no lasting effects, but it doesn't taste pleasant, can sting the eyes for a few seconds and hinders their sense of smell. Or if you prefer, carry a bottle of water with a sports cap, so that you can squirt at the dog coming at you. Your dog is your priority and you need to protect him or her. They need to be able to rely on you.

THE TEN COMMANDMENTS OF CITY DOG LIVING:

1. To walk your dog on a lead on the city's streets and pathways.

2. To be respectful of every other person and dog that shares the city with you.

3. Aim for you and your dog to be a great ambassador and show how well dogs can behave in shared spaces.

4. To learn what your dog does love about living in the city and use these to your advantage.

5. Be prepared for absolutely anything.

6. Keep your dog with you when it is off lead, there is no excuse for dogs charging up to other dogs even if they are friendly.

7. Always carry more than one poo bag.

8. Always carry treats and toys so that you can use every situation as an opportunity for training.

9. To respect your dog's and other dogs' boundaries.

10. Set yourself up for success in terms of choosing the right breed and creating the right environment for you both.

11.

HOLIDAYS

If you live in an amazing city like Sydney then, to my mind, each beach walk must be like a mini holiday. When the sun is shining, it must be the most amazing urban environment in which to be a dog owner – you have the best of both worlds. For most of us living in the city, a big expanse of sea, sand and the freedom to run is reserved for our weekends or holidays.

Before you take on a dog it is worth thinking about what your plans will be for holidays when you have a four-legged friend who is totally reliant on you. It may be that you have parents or a close friend who will take on the care. If this isn't the case, then holiday care can be very expensive.

KENNELS

Kennels are usually the cheapest option. Most kennels will consist of an inside and outside area where the dog is kept in isolation. The quality and standard of kennels varies greatly. You need to do your research and you need to 'drop in' to do checks before even thinking about putting your dog there. It is also worth asking how much exercise they will receive, as some kennels will not walk the dogs in their care – instead, they may have a field that they let them into once a day, or not at all. Others will do whatever you ask and pay for. However, if your dog is a pet that lives in your home, sleeps in comfort and is part of a family, most will find being kennelled extremely stressful and not enjoyable.

DOG-SITTER

Dog-sitters have become hugely popular, as most often your dog will go and live in their home. In theory this is a great idea, but you need to know all about the sitter, visit their home and know what a day will consist of for your dog. Ask sitters for references, check they are insured and that your dog is happy to be with this person. Arrange some single night or weekend overnight stays to make sure your dog is familiar with their environment and to iron out any teething problems before you leave the country.

My ideal option is to find a dog-sitter who will live in your own home, if you can afford it. It means that everything stays the same for your dog: their home, their bed, their meal-times, their walks and so on. The only difference is that their family have left the building! Your trusted dog walker will usually offer this as an additional service.

Before you go on holiday make sure that you have put some things into place:

· Notify your vet that you are away and give the vet's details to the carer.

HOLIDAY <u>WITH</u> YOUR DOG

Of course, you can take your dog on a trip with you. You can now find some amazing holiday homes that will welcome both of you. Just make sure that you take items such as dog towels, their bed and blankets, as most homes will not allow dogs on the furniture. You may also have to pay a one-off fee to some places for the dog to come with you.

If you are visiting an area where there are beaches nearby, do check the beach season rules as some areas are subject to dogs either not being allowed on the beach, only allowed on at certain times or during particular months. You do not want to be sorely disappointed when you lie your towel down to sunbathe and you get ushered off the beach!

Do consider that if the beach is a rare or new occurrence in your dog's life, you will need to show her what you expect of her in this situation. Do not just expect her to lie there all day. Do also provide shade, a secluded rest area and fresh water.

Lastly, do remember that if you are in a rural area, you usually still need to pick up your dog's poo. The sand is certainly not an excuse to ignore it. No one wants to be building a dog-poo-covered sandcastle.

· Put your dog's microchip number into your phone, so you have it to hand if for any reason it is required.

· Stock up on the food, ingredients, supplements and medication that your dog requires.

· Make sure that the dog's collar tag has the carer's details and phone numbers on them. There is no point your details being on there if you are holidaying in Brazil and in a totally different time zone.

· If your dog finds you leaving them stressful, the Bach Flower Remedy tincture of walnut can be great for helping with change.

· You can also leave your dog with an item of clothing that smells of you, such as a used pillow case or pyjama top in their bed.

THE CONTRACT OF DOG OWNERSHIP

When you take on a dog your life is going to change, big time.
In my opinion, this is the contract that you enter into with
your prospective new housemate.

I WILL PROMISE TO:

- Exercise, stimulate and get you out of the house for
  at least two hours every day.
- Keep you safe.
- Feed you food that will make you thrive.
- Give you fresh water.
- Keep you warm and give you shelter.
- Provide you with mental stimulation to keep you occupied.
- Not leave you alone for more than four hours at a time.
- Teach you how to behave.
- Learn to understand what you are trying to tell me.
- Never use physical punishment or painful techniques on you.
- Be the best, most fun, companion you could hope for.

As you can tell, it takes a lot of work to achieve all of this. So before you
dash out and purchase a dog, think about how you are going to achieve
all of this, how much it will cost you, what sacrifices you will need to
make and whether you are actually prepared for all of this. If you go
ahead and get it right, dog ownership is truly rewarding.

CONCLUSION: THE PATH OF DOG OWNERSHIP

Our lives with our dogs will take twists and turns, they will have good times and bad times, just as with any other relationship. As so often with relationships, the more you put in, the more you get out.

To build the best relationship with your city dog, remember that our four-legged friends are reliant on our ability and motivation to get them out of the house, to entertain them and to look after them.

If you have chosen the right breed for your lifestyle in your glorious city, then over time you should start reaping the rewards. As we get to know and understand our dogs, the easier the path of dog ownership becomes. We can begin to second guess their movements and reactions, and they ours. We become a dream team of six legs, trotting the concrete urban streets and making the most of our lives in these noisy parts.

A well-trained city-suited dog is a delight, they take it all in their stride. Of course there will still be things that they dislike and don't enjoy, but you should be well versed in what these are and how to respond.

Most of all, when you treat your dog with the kindness and respect it deserves, you will find their progress faster and a true joy to behold. Your confidence in them will soar and so will their responsiveness to you.

In short, we are looking to create well-balanced dogs with great city-dwelling owners who take the time to know about their dog. Every dog is different and it is up to you as an owner to pinpoint these to enjoy a long and happy adventure together.

I hope this book encourages you to tread your path carefully, with love, and to never stop learning. Dogs can teach us huge amounts and they never, ever cease to amaze me.

'Sometimes my dog winks at me, I always wink back, just in case it is some kind of code that I'm not aware of.'

SUPPLIERS

BEDS

Bone & Rag
www.boneandrag.com

Cath Kidston
www.cathkidston.com

ChillSpot
www.chillspot.biz

Mungo & Maud
www.mungoandmaud.com

Tuffies
www.tuffies.co.uk

BOWLS

Becobowl
www.becothings.com

Bone&Rag
www.boneandrag.com

Hunter
www.hunter.de

Mason&Cash
www.masoncash.co.uk

Kyjen
www.shop.kyjen.com

COLLARS

Bone & Rag
www.boneandrag.com

Friendly Dog Collars
www.friendlydogcollars.co.uk

Holly&Lil
www.hollyandlil.co.uk

Orvis
www.orvis.co.uk

Wonderdog
www.wonderdognyc.com

DOG COATS

Barbour
www.barbour.com

Equafleece
www.equafleece.co.uk

JACKETS (FOR HUMANS)

Barbour
www.barbour.com

Carhartt
www.carhartt.com

Canada Goose
www.canada-goose.com

Uniqlo
www.uniqlo.com

LEADS

CLIX leads sold widely in pet shops
and online

Found My Animal
www.foundmyanimal.com

Hiro and Wolf
www.hiro-and-wolf.com

Holly&Lil
www.hollyandlil.co.uk

WELLIES

Barbour
www.barbour.com

Dr. Martens
www.drmartens.com

Julia Lundsten for Nokian
www.nokianbyjulialundsten.com

Redwings
www.redwingshoes.com

FURTHER READING

Dr Ian Billinghurst, *Give Your Dog A Bone*,
    Warrigal Publishing, 1993
Henrietta Morrison, *Dinner for Dogs*,
    Ebury Press, 2012

ABOUT THE AUTHOR

Louise Glazebrook's lifelong love affair with dogs started from a very young age when she fell in love with a neighbour's golden retriever.

She is now a dog behaviourist, trainer and the founder of The Darling Dog Company in London. As well as running classes and offering one on one sessions, she works with youth offenders and prisoners to encourage and teach responsible dog ownership. She is mother to two children and the owner of one dog.

ACKNOWLEDGEMENTS

For my husband Kyle and my son Forest, you are my little dream team.

For my Ma, Pa and my sister Carly who have never doubted me and have helped with babysitting and lots of love.

There are friends who stick out like sore thumbs because they have been so wonderful. My best friends Kit De Luca and Mouse House (who by now must be bored of me), and Dan who never falters when I ask him his opinion yet again!

Kate Pollard, the most wonderful editor you could ever dream of. Working with her and Ping Zhu has been the best experience for which I am forever grateful. Thank you to Clare Skeats for designing such a beautiful book, and to Jane Graham Maw, a super literary agent and new dog owner.

To John Rogerson, the dog trainer. Without him I'm certain this book wouldn't have been possible.

Lastly, I have to mention some of the wonderful dogs who have made me the person I am today, and who have taught me so much, and remind me that there is always more to learn.

Cookie Dog, the best unicorn ever who I love so much; Gus, the original black Labrador who really set the wheels in motion for me, and Mr Happy Henry, the hardest foster dog I've ever had to give up. Then there's Ruby who taught me so much about dog-to-dog interactions; Toffee & Fudge for being so damn different from each other, and Sammy for teaching me just how crucial exercise is to a dog.

Lastly to all my clients, their dogs and their puppies I've worked with over the years, in some way you have all contributed to this book. As have all the dogs I've met through the stray kennels and the Dogs Trust work I do.

And to all the cafés, bakeries, and pubs that have kept me supplied in coffee, pain au chocolat, and wine, I thank you from the bottom of my heart.

INDEX

A
American Apparel 51
anal glands 83
autumn 54

B
Barbour 32, 49, 50, 138
barking 14
beaches 134
beagles 16
Becobowl 31, 138
beds 27-8
bitches, seasons 40, 41-2
biting 82, 90-2
boats, travelling on 125-6
Boden 51
Bone & Rag 28, 29, 31, 138
bones 70, 71
boots, for dog walkers 50
Border collies 13-14
border terriers 16
boredom 47
bowls, food 30-1
breeders 21-3
breeds, choice of 12-17
buses, travelling on 123, 125

C
Canada Goose 49, 139
Carhartt 49, 139
cars, dogs in 33, 126
Cath Kidston 28, 138
cavalier King Charles 16
chewing 91-3
children
 and breeds of dog 14
 socialisation with 119-20
ChillSpot 28, 138

city life 12-14
CLIX leads 30, 139
clothes, for dog walks 48-51
coats
 for dog walkers 49
 for dogs 32, 51
 fur 82-3
 collars 28-9
communication 105-11
contract of dog ownership 135
cooking food 69, 73, 75
crates 27, 28

D
dachshunds, miniature 16
dangerous dogs 126-8
day-care 61-2, 63
dehydrated food 71
docking tails 83
dog-sitters 133-4
dog trainers 97
dog walkers 62-3
dogs homes 25-6
dried food 71
Dr.Martens 50, 139

E
ears 81, 111
entertainment 55-6
Equafleece 32, 138
equipment 27-32
exercise 14, 47-8
 see also walks
eyes 79, 81, 110

F
first-aid kit 42-3
food 30
 for health problems 72
 quantity 71
 recipes 73, 75

food cont.
 tips 71-2
 toxic 72
 types of 69-72
food bowls 30-1
Found My Animal 30, 139
French bulldogs 15
Friendly Dog Collars 29, 138
fur 82-3

G
games 47, 55-6, 100
gates 32
great Dane 16
greyhounds 15
grooming 14, 51

H
harnesses 29-30
hearing 81
Hiro and Wolf 30, 139
holidays 133-4
Holly&Lil 29, 30, 138
home alone 11-12, 62
home visits, vets 37
hormones 40-1
hot weather 52, 54
Hunter 31, 138

I
ID tags 28-9

K
kennels (when away) 133
Kyjen 31, 138

L
labradors 16
leads 30
Lhasa apso 16

Dog About Town by Louise Glazebrook

First published in 2014 by Hardie Grant Books

Hardie Grant Books (UK)
5th & 6th Floors
52-54 Southwark Street
London SE1 1RU
www.hardiegrant.co.uk

Hardie Grant Books (Australia)
Ground Floor, Building 1
658 Church Street
Melbourne, VIC 3121
www.hardiegrant.com.au

British Library Cataloguing-in-Publication Data. A catalogue record for this book is available from the British Library.

ISBN: 978-1-74270-775-4

Publisher: Kate Pollard
Senior Editor: Kajal Mistry
Editors: Charlotte Cole and Nicky Jeanes
Designer: Clare Skeats
Cover and Internal illustrations © Ping Zhu
Author photograph © Gerrard Charles Gethings
Indexer: Sharon Redmayne
Colour Reproduction by p2d

Printed and bound in China by 1010

10 9 8 7 6 5 4 3 2 1